PORTUGAL

BONECHI

© Copyright by CASA EDITRICE BONECHI
Via Cairoli 18b - 50131 Firenze, Italia
Fax +39 0555000766 - E-mail: bonechi@bonechi.it - Internet: www.bonechi.it

Publication created and designed: Casa Editrice Bonechi
Editorial management: Serena de Leonardis
Cover: Laura Settesoldi
Text by Rui Coimbra; Paolo Piazzesi: *page 5;* Patrizia Fabbri: *pages 8-12, 76-79, 107-110;*
Emília Ferreira *and* Jorge Cabello: *pages 114-118*
Translation: Elisabeth Plaister, *except pages 5-12, 76-79, 107-110:* Julia Weiss Goldin; *114-118.*
Map: Stefano Benini

Printed in Italy by Centro Stampa Editoriale Bonechi - Sesto Fiorentino.

*The majority of the photographs are property of the Casa Editrice Bonechi Archives. They were taken by Jean Charles Pinheira;
Andrea Fantauzzo: pages 6-7; Paolo Giambone: pages 8 above, 118 above; Luigi Di Giovine: pages 88, 90 below, 92 below,
94 below, 97, 98, 100, 101, 103, 112 below, 116 above, 118 center and below; EDITORIAL SOFOTO, LDA/Paulo Sotero:
117 center and below; photographs kindly supplied by Arquivo Nacional de Fotografia - INSTITUTO PORTUGUÊS DE MUSEUS:
pages 8 center and below, 9 below, 10 above.*

*Other photographs were provided by Atlantide/Massimo Borchi: pages 114, 115 above, 116 center and below, 117 above;
Jean Charles Pinheira: pages 9 above and center, 11-12, 107-110;
Paulo Sotero: pages 10 below, 76-77.*

*The publisher apologizes for any unintentional omissions. We would be pleased to include any appropriate acknowledgments
of which we are informed in subsequent editions of this publication.*

ISBN 88-476-0790-6

* * *

PREFACE

Facing the Atlantic, Portugal listens to the sea as to a long-standing friend in whom we have become accustomed to confiding, one who speaks to us by signs, knowing that these will be readily understood in the unique language understood only by ourselves. This relationship goes back a long way since the life of Portugal has always revolved around the sea, a fishing people in close contact with the waves, storms and ocean currents. The climate results from sea-bornet

winds and the heat which the privileged south enjoys in abundance. An invariably pleasant, Mediterranean atmosphere.

The fresh winters are followed by days of alternating sun and rain, prelude to the later, hotter days typical of mid-year. Portugal's isolation from the rest of Europe has been a constant factor, with the plains of Castile and the Pyrenees constituting virtually insurmountable obstacles in days of yore when neither roads nor means of transport existed. Lying in south western Europe at the ocean's edge, Portugal is a land of multiple landscapes, mountains and valleys in the north and centre making way for plains in more southerly latitudes. The entire coast is fringed with a succession of beaches, some small and backed by an amphitheatre of rock, others endless stretches of finest sand seeming to be bleached daily whiter by the transparency of the ocean waters.

And, as for the past, memory can barely encompass such a wealth of momentous events. The name Portugal almost certainly arose from that of a city situated on the estuary of the Douro River, a village of streets and houses inhabited by fishermen and life-long merchants. Portus Calle was the name by which it was christened by the Romans, later to become one of the busiest urban centres of the peninsula. This is today's Oporto, the country's second city, washed by the weary waters of the river winding between vine-laden hillsides, dwellings perched on the slopes, beneath a vault of unpredictable sky.

The north was likewise the cradle of the country that was created when a Prince of Burgundy was granted the regency of the County of Portucale, an honour upon which he did not hesitate to expand when he was struck by the notion to be king. Portugal — united around the talent and courage of her first king, Dom Afonso Henriques — became independent in 1143, though future events were to prove this triumph to be ephemeral. But, for the time being, Portugal had freed itself from Castile. The situation was reversed in 1580 when the linking of royal blood allowed a Spanish monarch to ascend the Portuguese throne. This monarch was Dom Felipe, first of three of the same name who were to impose their rule on the Portuguese until the mid-XVII century. Independence was won back in 1640, the preceding period constituting but a brief interregnum in national pride but, nonetheless, important enough to be set down in the pages of history and to brand the already sceptical nature of the people.

Wherever you go, you encounter sights dating back to distant eras, when the days passed slowly and every season was a cycle in itself. From time to time, the habitual tranquility is broken by feast days on which large processions devotely follow the statue of the patron saint standing on a flower-decked pedestal, devout festivals where the colours of the procession vie for attention with the hues of local china and regional costumes. On such occasions, the crowds gather to live every moment as though it were the last, knowing that another busy year must pass before the festivities can be repeated.

The old red of the roof tops stoop before the lofty church towers and the central squares welcome chattering groups as the sun descends in splendour over the horizon. Everywhere there are castles, grey stones methodically chiselled into shape to produce battlemented towers, solid ramparts, fortifications encircling villages which are genuine living museums. These constructions are landmarks on the path followed by the Christian kings in their struggle against the Moors, strategic points resounding with tales of princes and fairies, spots which the modern world has not shorn of their memories of warfare, names and places keeping alive a common geneological tree with roots burying deep into the north of Africa.

But this is not the only mark of courage recorded from the past. There were others in which daring was not the product of the suffering of war but of the pain of separation and distance. They were times of discovery in far seas, first the Atlantic islands of Madeira, the Azores and Cape Verde and, later, other continents. Contacts which were maintained over the centuries, as though the ocean had brought about precocious maritime relationships with ever more distant regions. The ships departing from Lisbon at the end of the XV century knew with certainty only that the sea held secrets to be discovered, that the bad weather waves dredged evil beings up from the depths, that the end of the world lay somewhere beyond the horizon. But the months passed between sea and sky held less terrible surprises for these sailors. Even before the century turned, Vasco da Gama rounded the Cape of Good Hope, allowing the Portuguese to reach the eastern coast of Africa and so on to India. In 1500 different routes were explored, leading to the discovery of Brazil, yet another continent and, implicitly, a new concept of the Earth, facts recorded by Manueline art in every monument erected during those days and glorified in inspried epic form by Camões in his "Lusiads", a long poem admirably expressing the saudosismo, the nostalgic yearning, inherent in the Portuguese character, faith as the driving force behind all action, the past excelling over anything the future might hold. And between those early days and the present so much has happened, vicissitudes of feast and famine, joy and sadness, boom and dispair, such as was experienced in Lisbon at the time of the great earthquake in 1755, providing Pombal with the chance to build a new city while saving the country from economic decline. But the country was to be subjected to further suffering, on the dawn of the new century. Portugal was invaded by Napoleon's armies, occasioning years of profound desperation. The revolution of 1910 made way for the Republic, with the royal family and aristocracy departing for exile in Great Britain. The following years of unstable government were ended by the dictator's coup in 1926, allegedly to save the economy and instituting policies which were to isolate Portugal from Europe and the rest of the world. Plural democracy was established by events beginning in April 1974 after decades of obligatory and absurdly proud isolation to which the Portuguese people were forcibly subjected.

Events, every one, to test a nation's strength of character. But, surprisingly, this political and social diet appears not to have affected the Portuguese nature, one of mingled melancholy and passion, lowered eyes and open heart, tears provoked by the sad plaint of fado song flowing together with tears of joy. As though, when all is said and done, these facets, being the most genuine, were stored in the deepest recesses of the Portuguese soul, out of reach of external reality.

AZULEJOS

Although its origins are Moorish, and it was the Moors who brought the *azulejos* to Europe, these beautiful tiles did indeed find a second home in the Iberian Peninsula. Here they not only took root, but they developed into a true art. Ever since the sixteenth century these elaborate tiles have been used to decorate exteriors and interiors including floors and ceilings, and have been made in astonishingly large sizes especially in Portugal. The inhabitants of this country immediately demonstrated a particular fondness for this type of decoration.

The *azulejos* decorations quickly left an indelible imprint on the physiognomy of entire towns and became an authentic trait of Portuguese architecture. As the centuries passed, however, not even these artistic tiles could escape the influence of changing tastes. Thus, even though the more specifically Renaissance motifs dominated sixteenth century *azulejos*, along with the geometric patterns that are more directly linked to the Moorish tradition, the transition to Mannerism and then the Baroque left its mark on 17th and 18th century production with increasingly elaborate scenes, greater attention to naturalistic detail and polychrome, that gradually came to dominate over the more usual two-color motifs in white and blue with a few, discreet touches of yellow here and there.

In the nineteenth century, with the advent of neoclassicism the *azulejos* went into a decline Then, in the early twentieth century they enjoyed a dazzling rebirth when Portuguese Art Nouveau found a medium of expression that fit perfectly with its esthetics in these decorated, colorful tiles.

In the meantime, however, even the production methods had evolved. And yet, the greatest progress took place during the sixteenth century when the majolica technique was introduced allowing the skilled artisans to paint their designs directly on the tile prior to firing, without causing the heat of the kilns to damage the colors.

Azulejos was becoming a true art unto itself to which countless talented artists would dedicate their skills. We can mention the great Antonio de Oliveria Bernardes a master who lived between the sixteenth and seventeenth centuries, and left us true masterpieces. His traditional blue and white tiles were technically perfect and of astonishing size. His son, Policarpo was famous for elaborate decorative cycles.

Azulejos is considered an art, as borne out by the many modern artists who work on the them, and mainly the fact that the city of Lisbon has dedicated a museum to these elegant tiles that are symbol of Portugal.

The **Museu Nacional do Azulejo** is housed in the sixteenth century *Convento di Madre de Deus*, founded by the widow of Joao II.

Here, in strictly chronological order we can follow the history and marked transition of these items from crafts to art.

Panels, photographs and examples reveal the levels of expression to

Previous page, above, an azulejos panel outside an antique bookshop in the Chiado District. Center and bottom, two panels displayed in the Museu Nacional do Azulejo of Lisbona: the coat of arms of the Duke of Braganza (27 x 54 cm) dated 1558 and a 17th century panel of tiles with a square motif (209 x 95.7 cm.).

On this page, top and center, three azulejos panels that decorate the Santaréem market and a decorative panel at the Pinhao railroad station; below, a detail of the Terreiro do Paco on an azulejos panel depicting Lisbon prior to the 1755 earthquake (111.5 cm high), in the Museu Nacional do Azulejo of Lisbon.

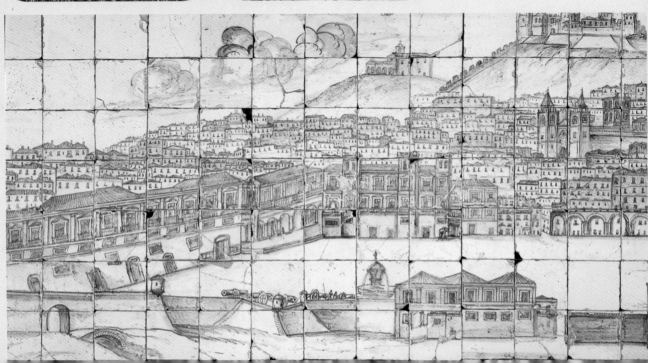

St. Luke, detail of the sixteenth century altarpiece in the church of Nossa Senhora da Vida, comprising 1384 tiles depicting a scene from the Nativity (500 x 465 cm.).

A vase of flowers on a panel (185 x 142 cm) from the former convent of N.S. da Esperança in Lisbon (17th cent.) in the Museu Nacionale do Azulejo in Lisbon.

Below, colorful azulejos decorate a bench in the Palácio Fronteira gardens in Lisbon.

which the *azulejos* can rise. It is sufficient to mention a single splendid example: the large eighteenth century panel that dominates the wall of the cloister with an incomparable image of Lisbon prior to the devastating earthquake of 1775.

FEAST DAYS AND FESTIVALS

Often, when speaking of Portugal and its people we tend to think of sadness and melancholy almost as if this were the main and most intimate trait. Perhaps this derives from the *Fado*, the traditional Portuguese music that originated in Africa.

Known and loved throughout the world, grief and sadness are the leitmotifs of this music. For centuries, more than anything else, *Fado* – the word comes from the Latin *fatum* "destiny" – has expressed the fatalism typical of a country troubled by emigration, and the desperation of a poor district, the sadness of a worker's life without any hopes for the future. Over time, however, it has become an art, and like every art it has had its masters, first among them the magnificent Amalia Rodrigues who passed away recently. And yet, aside from these nostalgic, beautiful melodies, Portugal is famous for its countless, grandiose and colorful folk festivals.

Many of these festivals have their roots in the country's earliest history and often they are held in honor of some saint, or to celebrate certain events such as the coming of spring or the end of the harvest. Thus, illuminated processions, sumptuous dinners and folk dances are held year after year, in any season and in the most diverse places throughout the country. And so, the procession of ornamental carts is held on the fourth Sunday of Lent at Mafra near Lisbon ; to celebrate the *Festa dei Terceiros* during Holy Week there are countless processions that also mark the solemn beginning of the bullfighting season in Portugal. The livestock fairs boom in spring as do the "tournaments" that are held in conjunction with them, and in parallel there is an infinity of Flower Festivals such as the famous one in Madeira.

The summer is dedicated to *Festas* in honor of Sao Joao (St. John) and Sao Pedro (St. Peter) that fall on the 24th and 29th of June, respectively.

The liveliest celebrations for the first are held in Port and

Braga, for the latter in Lisbon as well as in smaller towns proving the popularity of these saints.

Another highly popular event is the *Festa do Colete Encarnado*, the first weekend in July at Vila Franca de Xira. The men all wear a red waistcoat in honor of the costume traditionally worn by the Cavaliere di Ribatejo to whom bullfights and bull races are dedicated; and the *Festa dos Tabuleiros* that is held at Tomar on Pentecost, every two or three years. Amidst singing, dancing and bullfights, 400 girls walk in a procession each balancing a tray of about thirty loaves on their heads.

In August it is time for the historic *Romaria de Nossa Senhora da Agonia*, at Viana do Castelo on the third Sunday of the month. It is a festival that centers around a traditional and very crowded religious procession, the blessing of all the fishing boats, marching bands, fireworks and a bullfight on the Saturday closest to 20 August.

Other famous processions are dedicated to *Nossa Senhora dos Remédios*, on 8 September at Lamego, with a large Triumphal Procession that includes carts decorated with biblical scenes, and *Nossa Senhora da Nazaré*, that is held on the same day at Nazaré.

And if in summer there is a myriad of celebrations dedicated to the sea and fishing, in autumn, the protagonists are wine and livestock with many famous fairs throughout the country.

Two shots of the bullfighting at Póvoa de Varzim. Portuguese bullfights are seemingly less bloody than the Spanish version: the bull's horns are blunted and covered with leather sheaths; and the animals are never killed in the arena before the spectators' eyes.

Bulls are the main attraction of the *Feira de Outubro* that is held the first of October at Vila Franca de Xira, where the bulls run through the streets in addition to the "classic" bullfights. *Folk*, with its many facets, is the focus of an authentic *Festa Nacionale* that is held in Algarve. Then come the traditional celebrations of All Saints' Day, Christmas, New Years and Carnival with special attention to the two weeks between 25 December and 6 January, that is the *Festa dos Rapazes* when the streets of Bragança are crowded with young people in fancy dress. It is almost as if to say that all Portugal, a land of ancient beloved customs, swarms with *Festas* – with many more than we have mentioned here to prove that the country's soul is not always melancholy. In fact it is profoundly inclined to celebrations – for the faith, and for love of its own history and traditions.

Above, students from the University of Coimbra during the "Queima das Fitas" (the burning of the ribbons) festival, a seven hundred year old tradition. The university faculties are identified by differently colored ribbons, and at the end of the academic year the ribbons are burned in a huge cauldron.

Center and bottom: two glimpses of one of the liveliest romàrias, *the festival of Nossa Senhora da Agonia at Viana do Castelo, with three days of singing, dancing, music, processions, bullfights and fireworks.*

A TASTE OF PORTUGAL

Power to the clichés! With but few exceptions, most foreigners are convinced that aside from a certain skill in preparing beans (*feijão*), Portuguese cooking begins and ends with codfish (*bacalhau*)…fried, poached, baked and what have you. Tradition maintains that there are 365 recipes, one for every day of the year! And although we are delighted to propose one of them to honor the customs - the highly original *Codfish with Paprika* – we must emphasize the fact that Portuguese cuisine is as vast and varied as the country's landscape. You can feel the Atlantic breezes, hear the babbling rivers and streams, and the rustling leaves in the orchards, olive groves and vineyards; you can recognize the elegance of *azulejos*, the charms of the Portuguese Gothic, the passion of the *fado* – the folksongs and the wit of Pessoa.

Portuguese cuisine, that is traditionally "poor", genuine and wholesome, loves strong flavors, and aromas (such as the *Roast Lamb*, the recipe is on these pages) and fish and meat combinations. In each dish, ancient folk knowledge combines with the pride of noble traditions. In addition to Minho that gives us the "national" dish, a soup known as *Caldo verde* (the recipe is here too), there is the northern Tràs-os-Montes region with its robust cuisine that combines the *caldo de couves com feijão* (cabbage and bean soup), with hearty dishes such as *Feijoada à transmontana* or refined ones like *trutas* (trout) *à mode de Barrosa*. Famous for its cheeses, orchards and oil, Beira Baixa offers simple and tasty foods such as *sopa de abòbora com fios de ovos* (squash soup with scrambled eggs) and *coelho com carqueja* (one of the

most delectable ways of preparing rabbit), to conclude with the famous *tigelada* (a cream dessert) or *migas dolces* (sweet soups). In the Beira Litoral district, where Coimbra is located, the wealth of the natural landscape is reflected in the foods. The typical dishes include *sopa seca de nabiças* (broccoli and pasta), *ensopada de enguias* (eel soup) and *leitao à Bairrada* (suckling pig from Bairrada). The vast assortment of sweets and pastries also has its special highlights such as *ovos moles* the famous dessert from Aveiro that is made from eggs, sugar and cinnamon. Estremadura, the region behind Lisbon is famous for its seafoods, lobsters and the outstanding wines from Colares. In addition to the famous pork dish, Alentejo offers light and tasty seafood: along with the famous *açorda alentejaja*, a fish broth and bread soup with garlic, olive oil and coriander, we must not overlook *açorda com pescada e améijoas* (codfish and clam soup) and *migas alentejanas* (a bread soup). The Algarve, with its sunny beaches bounded by lush orchards makes its own statement, with the best version of *caldeirada*, the classic fish soup made with garlic, vegetables, tomatoes and peppers (we present that recipe as well), and the *sopa de conquilhas* (seafood soup), *améijoas na cataplana* (a version of paella with pork, mollusks, ham and onions) and *choquinhos com tinta* (inky shellfish). And the traditional almond cake, *fatia de bolo de améndoa com gila* is absolutely irresistible.

The wines are abundant and famous. Porto, produced in the Douro valley is certainly among the most renowned: dry or sweet, white, red and blond, aged for long years and strong, it is fine for dessert – or thought. The *vinhos verdes* from Minho are delicious. The name has nothing to do with the color since 70% is a lively red that can accompany an entire meal and the rest is white: the "green" means that it is aged only a very short time. The wines from the Moncao district are also just as famous. The Dao and Lafoes areas produce velvety reds and whites that can stand up to comparisons with the famous rosés and reds from the Algarve. And to finish, the spectacular Madeira wines are perfect for the eclectic and refined dishes from that island.

CALDO VERDE

500 gr/1 lb potatoes
200 gr/1/2 lb savoy cabbage
1 large onion
2 cloves garlic
1 "chorizo"
or regular sausage
olive oil
salt

In a large saucepan combine 1 1/2 liters/1 1/2 quarts water, 3-4 tablespoons olive oil, add the sausage, and the peeled potatoes, onions and garlic; cook over a medium flame for 20 minutes. When done, put the potatoes, onions and garlic through the food mill (or blender) and save the cooking liquid. Slice the sausage, put the strained mixture back into the cooking liquid, add the cabbage and salt and cook for another 20 minutes. Put a slice of sausage in each individual bowl, top with a drop of olive oil and then pour the hot soup over it all.

ROAST LAMB

1.5 kg/ 3 lbs lamb
(saddle, shoulder or leg)
1/4 liter/1 cup red wine
1 large onion
4 cloves garlic
1 bay leaf
1 teaspoon paprika

1 teaspoon cumin seeds
1 handful of parsley
12 thin slices of bacon
1 "chorizo" or dry, spicy sausage
olive oil
pepper
salt

In a saucepan (terracotta is preferable if you have one), combine the sliced onion, chopped parsley, the bay leaf, cumin, wine salt and pepper. Add the meat – cut into pieces and arrange it so that the marinade covers it midway. Put the bowl in a cool place for 24 hours and turn the meat frequently. The next day, remove the lamb from the marinade; make a cut in each piece and stuff with a rolled up slice of bacon.
Put the meat back into the marinade, add 2 tablespoons olive oil, set the oven to 180° C/350° F and bake for around 2 hours. At the midpoint, turn the meat so that it uniformly coated with the marinade; 10 minutes before the baking time is up, add the sliced sausage.

CODFISH
WITH PAPRIKA

700 gr/1 1/2 lbs codfish
500 gr/1 lb potatoes
500 gr/1 lb tomatoes
4 medium onions
4 cloves garlic
2 bay leaves
parsley
paprika
pepper
salt

Rinse, skin and fillet
the codfish; slice the potatoes, tomatoes and onions; crush the garlic. In a
skillet, arrange the tomatoes, onions,
codfish, garlic and potatoes in layers,
season with salt and pepper; sprinkle
the top layer with chopped parsley
and bay leaves, half a teaspoon of paprika and a squiggle of olive oil.
Cover and cook slowly for about 45
minutes.

CALDEIRADA DE PEIXE

1 kg/2 lbs conger eel
500 gr/1 lb calamari
500 gr/1 lb clams
2 tomatoes, peeled and cubed
2 or 3 medium onions
1 clove garlic

1/2 glass grappa
pili-pili sauce
parsley, chopped
olive oil
pepper
salt

Chop the garlic and onion, and cook slowly in a little
olive oil until barely golden, add the tomatoes and parsley. Cook for ten minutes then add 1 liter/1 quart water,
the grappa, the eel and calamari, all cut into pieces, add a
few drops of pili-pili sauce and salt and pepper to taste.
When it comes to the boil, lower the flame, and cook covered for twenty minutes. Finally, uncover, add the clams and
cook over a lively flame for another 10 minutes. Serve with
boiled potatoes.

Two pictures of the fortified town.

VALENÇA

Right on the Spanish border, in the north of Portugal, lies Valença, a town which grew up on the Roman road linking the city of Braga with the towns of **Lugo**, **Vigo** and **Santiago de Compostela**. On account of its location on the border, on the left bank of the Minho River, the town always played an important role in the defence of territorial boundries against the Spaniards who are here so close at hand. The conflicts with the kingdom of Leon in the XIII century and also later in the XVII century during the Restauration War, tested the defence capacity of Valença against the onslaught of foreign troops.

Even today, the warring activities of Valença are readily apparent in the physical layout of the town, with ramparts protecting the historical centre which may be entered through one of the many gates in the sturdy fortifying walls. The town is today divided into two distinct parts. Inside the walled area are rows of two or three storey houses lining narrow streets which mark the divisions between the different quarters. This area contains the churches, administrative buildings, the pillory. The more modern additions, including the tourist and commercial activities inherent in the life of any border town, developed outside the walls, spreading untrammelled through the open country which has, since time immemorial, been fed by the river dividing Spain and Portugal.

The exterior of the Parish Church and the statue of Christ, inside the church.

CAMINHA

Originally, Caminha was situated on an island between the Coura and Minho rivers, separated from the shore by only a short distance when the tide was low, owing its development to trade downriver towards the estuary. The town gained a degree of notoriety with the expulsion of the Moors, during the period of the Christian Reconquest which saw a succession of declines, destruction and invasions and a slow rebirth from the ashes. During the XIV century, with the strengthening of trade links between Portugal and the countries of Northern Europe, Caminha started to expand, even beyond its walls dating from the beginning of the millennium which had, until then, restricted the development of the town.

Nowadays, Caminha devotes itself almost exclusively to trade and tourism. Its visiting cards are the **Igreja Matriz** (Collegiate Church) built between 1488 and 1565, endless gardens, pine woods and beaches. The solid **Fortaleza de Insua** was a convent for six hundred years and now stands as an isolated ruin on a rocky islet, refusing however to disappear altogether in its determination to witness what the modern day brings.

The picturesque village of Lindoso.

VIANA DO CASTELO

Viana do Castelo reclines on the banks of the Rio Lima and spreads through the green-decked valley, close by the sea and the hill of Santa Luzia. The city is almost entirely flat, cut into virtually geometrical shapes by streets, intersected by lanes, squares, nooks of unique and vivid character. Here and there amid the cluster of houses rise palatial homes, such as the **Palácio dos Távoras**, today occupied by the local council offices, buildings with original designs that never cease to amaze.

To visit this city is indisputably to plunge into a living museum of history. Dating from medieval times, the gothic style **Sé** (cathedral), the **Palacete dos Melos Alvins**, the **Casa dos Arcos**, not forgetting the **Casa das Caravelas**. Of the heritage from other centuries and later eras, special mention should be given to the **Igreja de São Domingos** from the mid-XV century, the **Fortress of São Tiago da Barra** with its baroque entrance, and the **Palácios de Rego Barreto** situated in the **Jardim de Dom Fernando**, built in the XVIII century.

One of the most pleasant surprises awaiting the visitor to this city is its main square, the Praça da República, offering an architectural conformation of monumental proportions: the buildings of the **Paços do Concelho** of manifestly medieval origin, the **Casa da Misericórdia** which is the city's most sumptuous renaissance monument and, in the centre of this square, the beautiful fountain with sculptured decorations on its several basins.

But the interest of Viana do Castelo is not confined to its architectural heritage. It is also a city of festivals and fairs, well-deserving of the name it was once given — the folklore capital. Indeed, anybody privileged to attend the Festa do Traje, taking place on the Sunday afternoon of the Romaria da Senhora da Agonia, will readily perceive the wealth of this region's folklore and arts and crafts at the sight of the pageantry involving over a thousand participants. A festival of music and traditional dancing steeped in colour, fire works and fair grounds, processions and a bull fight.

The nearby Monte de Santa Luzia, which may be ascended on foot, by cable car or by road, affords a panoramic view, one of the most spectacular of this Upper-Minho region. This look out point was chosen as the site of the **Basílica de Santa Luzia**, built in neo-Byzantine style during the early years of this century.

Viana de Castelo: view of the city and the façade
of the Basílica de Santa Luzia.

The interior of the Church of the Misericórdia.

Two views of Barcelos.

Braga: the Cathedral.

BARCELOS

Barcelos, situated on the right bank of the Rio Cávado, is the place which gave origin to the Portuguese symbol of the pottery cockerel of richly coloured plummage and proudly red comb, immortalized in the hand-crafted pottery figures which the artisans of the area do not tire of modelling. These and, indeed, many other arts and crafts consituting the ethnographical wealth of the region and which may be purchased in the numerous little gift shops or, alternatively, during the Festas de Maio (May celebrations) held annually and incorporating the Feira Grande (great fair), a popular festival gaily illuminated by thousands of lights and enlivened by the local wine and brightened by vast quantities of flower petals carpeting the ground around the magnificent **Igreja das Cruzes**, dating from 1704.

BRAGA

Bracara Augusta was the name of this town founded to serve as capital of the Roman province of Galecia, in the north west of the Iberian Peninsula, beside the mountains and facing the immensity of the ocean. It was rebuilt by the Catholic kings when they recovered it from Arab domination — during the course of which the city was totally destroyed in 711 — and was to function for many years as outpost of the Christian faith. Even today, this religious disposition is still apparent, one chapel succeeding another, numerous churches, local trade ever ready to provide the faithful with every type of object related to the Catholic religion: rosaries, candles, figures of Christ, finely embroidered scarves, holy cards and paintings.
Braga holds pride of place as regards the architectural treasures it presents to the visitor at every step. In the

19

centre of Praça do Município, opposite the **Palácio da Câmara**, the **Fonte do Pelicano** testifies to the artistic wealth of the city: it is in the baroque style and bears the coat of arms of the Archbishop Dom Gaspar of Bragança, belonging originally to the since demolished Convento dos Remédios. Likewise, the **Igreja de Falperra**, the **Palácio do Raio** and the **Palácio da Câmara**, the **Tibães altars** and the **Igreja dos Congregados** are all examples of finest baroque which the master-builders of the time succeeded in importing with upmost sensitivity from the Europe beyond the Pyrenees and, during the colonization period, transplanting to Brazil.

But Braga holds yet more artistic treasures: the **Sé** (cathedral), a real fortress of a church of Romanesque origin which, by its sheer size, dominates the entire centre of the city. The **Capela** and the **Casa dos Coimbras** — most noteworthy buildings erected in 1525 by Dom João de Coimbra, Provisor to Archbishop Dom Diogo de Sousa who had, for his part, had the Hospital and **Igreja de São Marcos** built in 1508 — also constitute an important

The hospital and the Church of São Marco.

Avenida Central: the Church of the Lapa and the Palace da Arcada.

The Fonte do Pelicano, in the middle of the Praça do Município and a view of the Casa dos Coimbras.

Exterior and interior of the Church of Bom Jesus do Monte.

part of the varied architectural heritage of the city.

A very pleasant walk, for instance, is through the leafy **Parque do Bom Jesus** lying on a hillside planted with broad-crowned trees on which was built the church of the same name and which may be reached by way of an imposing stairway. The atmosphere is idyllic indeed, with numerous fountains and an immense artificial lake ideal for leasurely boating.

The hall mark, however, of life in Braga is the religious nature of its traditions: should you visit the city at the end of June, it would be a great shame not to take part in the joyful festivities of the São João celebrations, two days during which people take to the streets for the sole purpose of enjoying themselves. The atmosphere is one of euphoria all along Avenida da Liberdade and the wide open spaces of the **Parque da Ponte**. The devotion of the local people is amply demonstrated in the numerous processions throughout the year, over and above the traditional ascent of Monte Sameiro and the devotions of Easter Week when the city is decked in light and the faithful erect altars in the streets.

GUIMARÃES

It would be unjust to limit Guimarães to its age-old castle, birthplace of the Kingdom of Portugal in its emancipation from Castile. The fortress is flanked by the **Igreja de São Miguel do Castelo**, the Paço dos Duques de Bragança and, lower down, the city with its many places of interest. A case in point is the Rua de Santa Maria, one of the most typical of the city, with its whitewashed fa-

On this page, and at the top of the opposite one, two views of the Palace of the Dukes of Bragança.

The Church of Nossa Senhora da Oliveira.

The cloister of the Museu de Alberto Sampaio.

The Church of Santos Passos.

The Castle and another view of the Palace of the Dukes of Bragança.

çades in tones of ochre, wooden balconies and sixteenth century doorways. Following this street to its end, we come to the the Largo da Oliveira, containing the **Paço do Concelho** (Old Town Hall) and the **Igreja de Nossa Senhora da Oliveira**, with the tower rising to the left of its magnificent façade and the immense blind window above the doorway. In the cloister, on romanesque lines of the mid-XIII century — and in the adjoining buildings — are to be seen works of art and historical documents which are the patrimony of the **Museu de Alberto Sampaio**. Behind this square lies the Praça de Santiago which is surely one of the most beautiful areas of the city with its sizeable collection of XVIII century houses. Here and there, instances of religious and lay architecture, such as the fine **Igreja dos Santos Passos** with its tapering, baroque style towers and typically Portuguese façade. Another is the **Paço dos Duques** (Ducal Palace), an imposing seigneurial residence inspired by French architecture of the genre, built in 1401 by the Conde de Barcelos, first Duque de Bragança.

The beaches and the port of Póvoa de Varzim.

PÓVOA DE VARZIM

Póvoa de Varzim may be considered a slowly emerging great city, a constantly developing urban centre involved in bustling activity carried on side by side with its traditional fishing and well-run tourism industry revolving around a large beach of fine sand irresistibly attracting all those eager to bathe in the sun and sea on offer virtually all year round.

However, not the whole of the town is caught up in this development drive. There is a district which, despite its proximity to Oporto, is nonetheless immune to the constant commotion to which modern-day cities are prone. This tranquil Póvoa is the oldest section of the city, filled with fine examples of XVIII and XIX century architecture in unadultered, heavy and richly ornate northern style, brightly coloured tiles lending balance to the whole. Then there is the Rua da Junqueira, where the locals

gather and peaceably stroll at dusk, lined with small shops linking the charming Praça do Almada with the beachfront.

It is however on days of religious celebration that the more traditionalist aspect of the Póvoa character is readily apparent. At such times, you almost forget that this is an industrial area with unbridled progress apparent in every building.

Whether the occasion is the Festa da Senhora da Lapa or the Festa de São Pedro — in fact, patron saint of fisherman — whether the Festa de São João or the Procissão dos Passos or the Procissão das Lanternas, everybody without exception takes to the streets to participate in the ceremonies. At such times, the visitor may watch fishermen preparing their delicious *caldeirada*, fish stew, richly decorated boats and great crowds holding candles, all cultural traditions from the distant past transmitted from generation to generation, struggling determinedly to counteract the threat of anonymity inherent in modernization.

Two views of the city.

OPORTO

This is the origin of the name of Portugal, claims the poet, echoing popular lore. Indeed, if we are to believe the writings of long ago and in the natural evolutionary processes of a language, it really is not so far-fetched to suppose that Portucale (now Oporto) could well have been the original name of this country. Oporto is a granite city, grey and mysterious on occasion, when the fog lowering over river and sea roll inland to cloak the city. City of hills harbouring tales in every one of the stones of which the buildings are constructed, medieval, baroque, nineteenth century, all contributing to Oporto's reputation as a city rich in architectural heritage. Centuries of superimposed history are, effectively, reality in perpetual motion, people who give the city an atmosphere of never-ending festivity, street hawkers everywhere, tables on the streets offering cosmetics, women calling aloud their wares of umbrellas, colour and sound erupting endlessly.

But there are gardens too, nooks of stillness in the urban anarchy, havens of greenery offsetting the dry and arid, ancient stone: the lime trees of the **Palácio da Cordoaria** and the **Jardim de S. Lázaro**, the cedars and palms, the dour cypresses, all seeming to help this hive of constant activity to breath. Each garden is a place of romance, like that at **Quinta da Macieirinha** with its rose garden rounding off a stroll down the narrow street bordered by walls draped in ferns and moss. In due season, the magnolia and camelia explode in effusive colour and Oporto is decked in yet greater glory. The river as seen from here bears witness to what is said, of oaths, pardons and promises, the gently but mighty flowing towards the yearned-for sea after its fraught passage between vineyards and mountains.

The riverside road confirms that Oporto's livelihood are indeed the river and the sea. As it carries the traveller along the banks of the Douro River to the rockstrewn sands of the Foz (estuary) beaches, glimpses are revealed of the remains of long-standing fishing activities, hulls consumed by the onward march of years of neglect, skeletons of boats, nets proclaiming a usefulness long disregarded. Meanwhile, fishermen fiddle absentmindedly with mooring rope as the sun sets or when the intense blue of the sky — a blue to be seen only in Oporto, in dramatic contrast to the frequent grey of its clouds heralds scalding heat.

With the changing of the times and the need to use larger

The Cathedral.

The Cloister and the Sacristy.

vessels, the nerve-centre of trade moved further afield, to Leixões, an industrial agglomeration rivalling Leça and Matosinhos. Nowadays the Douro is sailed only by vessels of shallow draught and in the **São João da Foz suburb** it is no longer the bustle of busy fishermen that is to be heard but rather the sedate speech of the most leisured citizens who currently reside here, having transformed this entire area — Boavista, Avenida do Brasil, Avenida de Montevideu, among others — into miniature Rivieras studded with open-air cafes and palatial homes surrounded by inviting gardens.

This is a city which upholds centuries-old tradition and only in this light may one understand its inhabitants who are deeply moved at the words: "antiga e mui nobre, sempre leal cidade invicta" — ancient and most noble, ever loyal and invincible city, words which justly sum up the noble character of its citizens.

SÉ DO PORTO

The **Sé** (cathedral) bears witness to the antiquity of Oporto, a city of long-standing architectural tradition with which the local people progressively enriched the city and modified the urban landscape. It is of Romanesque design dating from the second quarter of the XII century and extensively rebuilt during succeeding centuries. The façade is impressive indeed, boasting an ornate portal and rose window like an enormous iris lending charm to the whole. The two flanking towers are impressively domed, with battlements revealing defensive functions. The interior boasts mural paintings by Nicolau Nasoni and, upon entering the cloister, the visitor is treated to a rare example of Gothic architecture, a profusion of arches gaily compensating for the limited dimensions of this enclosed space.

The façade of the Church of Santo Ildefonso.

The statue of the "Infante D. Henrique".

IGREJA DE SANTO ILDEFONSO

This church, standing on the crest of a gentle hill, is of XVIII century origin. The façade reveals the marked influence of baroque artistic trends, with a multiplicity of elements on display to the visitor before entering the silence and seclusion of the church interior. Tiles deck the front walls, depicting scenes from the life of St Ildefonse and allegories of the Eucharist, accomplished artistry indeed, dating from 1932. Two towers rise steeply into the air and, between them, a projecting structure featuring a broad portico crowned by a triangular pediment. A seemingly endless flight of steps leads up to the church, the outside of which gives proof of considerable artistic creativity.

PRAÇA DA LIBERDADE

This is one of the largest and perhaps the prettiest square in Portugal. It is the true heart of Oporto residential, local government, business — or even for a pleasant stroll. In its centre stands the statue of Dom Pedro IV, close to **Avenida dos Aliados**, gazing down upon all that unfolds before his regal eyes.

On either side are buildings of carved façades, one succeeding the next, while one in particular appears to preside paternally over the whole square. This is the **Câmara Municipal** (Town Hall) with its tower in the *beaufroi* style rising from the centre of a broad and balanced façade. One end leads off towards the Trindade, Rua da Constituição and the select Boavista suburb. The other end of

The statue of Dom Pedro IV, in the centre of the Praça da Libertade.

The Torre da Igreja dos Clérigos.

the square gives onto a hill — ascent of which is considerably alleviated by the interest of the shop windows along the way — leading to the **Torre da Igreja dos Clérigos**, built between 1748 and 1763. It is a baroque structure which may safely be classified as the most original creation of the Italian architect Nasoni who is the author of a large part of the better religious architecture which the city of Oporto has to offer the visitor. It soars tier after tier, stairways climbed in their time without pause for breath, bold and elegant lines of an exuberant tower which, in would-be triumph, dominates the entire city. Nowadays, with the construction of one highrise after another, the Torre dos Clérigos is no longer set apart by its height. Only by its beauty. As Jorge de Sena says: "*para a minha alma eu pedia uma torre como esta, assim alta, assim de nevoa acompanhando o rio*" — for my soul would I desire such a tower, so tall, so hazy, attending upon the river.

The interior of the Church of São Francisco.

The Church "do Carmo" and a detail of the winged lion fountain.

IGREJA DE S. FRANCISCO

The **Igreja de S. Francisco** is like a cave containing incalculable riches, with gilded walls bearing evidence of painstaking artistry in every carved detail. This sacred precinct, which used to belong to the Franciscan friars, was built in 1233, although the church itself dates from 1383, having proved slow in the building since the architect was loath to risk failure in achieving the deserved grandeur of such a place of worship through undue haste. The visitor is greeted by a façade containing a magnificent XVII-XVIII century portal, while the southern wall is interrupted at regular intervals by Manueline style windows. Every inch of the interior is magnificent: altars, pillars, vaulting and columns radiate in all directions the dazzling light reflected from the windows on the gold leaf. The very atmosphere is pervaded by a spirit of opulence.

IGREJA DO CARMO

The **Igreja do Carmo** stands close to the winged lion fountain — in **Praça dos Leões** (Lion Square), one of the prettiest spots in Oporto, with a garden in which the palms counteract the horizontal plane of this large open space and monuments lend an added dignity. The church was built in the XVIII century in strict accordance with the rules of baroque. The façade is divided into three tiers, a number of statues adorn stone darkened by time and floral motifs add a note of lightness to the weight of the building.
The side wall is decorated with very fine tiles. The interior consists of a single nave lined by six altars. The main altar stands beneath a richly painted dome with a carved gilt altar piece dating from 1776.

The Moorish Hall, inside the Stock Exchange.

The interior of São Bento Station.

A side of the Chapel "das Almas".

SALÃO ÁRABE (MOORISH HALL)

Looking on to a square enclosed by beautiful buildings, the **Palácio da Bolsa** (Stock Exchange) appears to the visitor in all the solidity of its neo-classical style with the dark stone bringing into prominence the intersecting lines, the contours, columns and the tower crowning the entire building. From among the various large rooms that comprise the palace, the **Moorish Hall** deserves particular mention. It is a vast space richly decorated with Arab motives and was originally designed by Gustavo de Sousa. The ceiling, with its lacery in tones of blue, red and gold, hang above that magnificent oval salon — two stores high and in the writhing arabesque style.

ESTAÇÃO DE SÃO BENTO (SÃO BENTO STATION)

The entrance is magnificient, with is exceedingly high roof attempting to contain the voices of passengers calling out in their hurry and monumentary excitement. And on the walls — the real beauty of the place — tile panels in tones of blue and white, depict in a whole series lively scenes of the history of Portugal. The space, always busy and bustling, is rendered even more dynamic, for the daily humdrum activity — marked by the arrival of the trains and people rushing about — is added the epic and historic feeling of all those past heroes revealed by these tiles in the unequalled beauty of their delicate hues.

CAPELA DAS ALMAS

This chapel, built in the XVIII century, displays interesting *azulejos* panels on its façade and side wall. One of the most impressive panels depicts the *Death of St. Francis of Assisi*.

Two pictures of the Dom Luis Bridge.

THE BRIDGES OF OPORTO

The city is child of the river and the sea, elements which meet in the estuary and also, magically, by some virtually inexplicable symbiosis, in the air and in the nature of the inhabitants of this great city. The Douro River is as a mirror in which the people of Oporto glimpse their reflection when they look upon it from the windows of their homes or stroll down their steep streets towards the water's edge.

There are three bridges, each serving their respective part, of the city, each as useful as the next in their own different ways. Furthest from the estuary is the metal structure of the **D. Maria Bridge**, ever giving the impression of precarious balance, used by trains at all hours of the day and night, to the dismay of all using this mode of transport who cannot but fear that fate will not smile on them this time across. The leisurely pace at which the rail cars approach the upper carriageway allows ample time for unease to turn to outright anxiety and, when the train starts to cross the river, all passengers fall silent, intent

on the notion that the art of tightropewalking is being put to the test once more. But the bridge holds firm, despite the years it has had to bear its burden. Built in accordance with Gustave Eiffel's revolutionary precepts, the **D. Maria Bridge** consists of a single arch spanning the gorge in one giant stride. It is a metallic structure dangling in space like whimsical tracery, delicate as the filigree work of the north of Portugal.

The **D. Luis Bridge**, linking the centre of Oporto with the town of **Vila Nova de Gaia**, is likewise a broad arch but anchored to either bank by two roadways, the upper of which carries the heavy traffic crossing between the two towns divided by the river. Cars and motorbikes and pedestrians and public transport, a continual to-and-fro diminished but by the fall of night. But only for a few hours, because the people of Oporto are early risers and, when the sun peeks over the horizon, the **D. Luis Bridge** is already busy with the daily bustle of these hard-working people.

The third bridge, nearest the estuary, is of modern design, a heavier structure but equally elegant. This is the **Arrábida Bridge**, of reinforced concrete supporting a car-

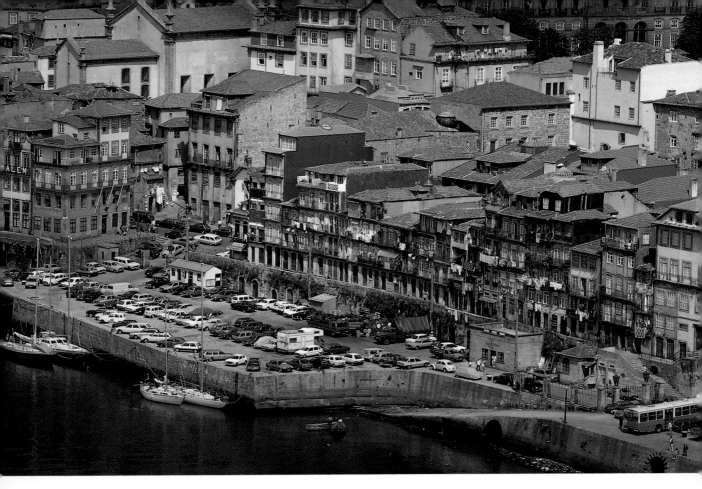

The port of the Ribeira district.

riageway offering views of both city and ocean. The visitor can from here get onto the riverside road, with the possibility of continuing to **Miragaia, Pasteleira** or **Passeio Alegre**. The beginning of a trip for some, the end of a lengthy journey for this river glittering as gold. In the evening breeze, when Oporto contrives to be more beautiful than ever, echo the verses of Gastão da Cruz:

Escutamos o Porto: os passos dados sobre as lajes, vozes soltas, feridas; falas num português perdido.
E ao teu encontro vem
A grande ponte sobre o rio.
O frio sobe do Douro,
A cidade expõe as suas luzes.
Escutamo-nos.

Let us harken to Oporto: steps sounding on the flags, stray voices, wounded; speech in a lost Portuguese
The great bridge over the river
Comes forward to meet you.
The cold rises from the Douro
The city shows its lights
Let us harken to them.

RIBEIRA

These are the most typical districts of the old borough, still retaining unchanged the old streets which seem to respect nothing, neither irregularities of the earth's surface, nor the most elementary rules of town planning. But what does that matter? The Ribeira (riverside) quarter is a magical maze of colours and scents, people sitting on their front door steps watching the world go by or craning their necks from an upstairs window to learn what the new day brings. This is the living image of Oporto the Eternal. The tall, narrow houses crowd one against the next oblivious of any human claustrophobia, alleys and squares that feel like wide open spaces after these dark passages. The atmosphere gives away what the local people are busy doing: the smell of washing causing immense, spotless sheets to appear hanging beneath every window, smoke billowing from an open doorway tells of a grilled sardine lunch, shouts from one building to the next carry the news of what is rife in the air.
To fully appreciate this scene, the visitor must cross to the other bank of the river, by way of the lower level of the Dom Luis Bridge. From this new view point, the misty waters of the Douro still manage to carry the harmo-

Picturesque houses at Ribeira.

nies and dissonances of this never-sleeping city. The scene is uncannily beautiful: the compact bank of buildings is punctuated by thousands of windows in constant activity, bright clothing swaying luxuriously in the sun, walls bearing witness to a past age, roofs scaling the hillside in tones of old tile red, church spires seeming to act as mainstays in precariously keeping this whole together. Although this scene is one of dark, grim hues in bad weather, it is well to remember that the impression is but transitory. It requires only that the cloud part to allow the sun to shine through for the area to undergo a complete transformation. Then, the incomparably blue sky vies with the fresh breeze blowing from the estuary and the smiles of the townsfolk, unforgettable spectacles on the banks of the peaceful river.

Ascending the hill a little way above the waters of the Douro, we reach a landscaped square, the Praça das Cercas (Enclosures Square), a name dating back to medieval times. This was the site of the enclosures of São Francisco and São Domingos, and also of the British Factory House (Feitoria Inglesa). The latter institution kept an eye on the extensive British interests in Oporto to which a number of subjects of that north European island kingdom had been attracted.

Today, the surrounding area is occupied by buildings of austere stone darkened by the passing of the years, lending the neighbourhood a weight denoting the antiquity of the place, a pervading atmosphere of avidity for trade existing at the beginning of the century which lead to the construction of distinguished residences for merchants and premises for trading and shipping companies. One side is occupied by the elegant **Palácio da Bolsa** (Stock Exchange) with its beautiful, delicate **Salão Árabe** (Moorish Hall) its decoration the product of an unbridled flight of the imagination. On the opposite side of the square stands the **Ferreira Borges market**, consiting of elegant metallic structures supporting the glass through which the sun pours untrammelled.

But the old market doubtless still remembers the bustle of vendors on market day though now it looks placidly down on less strenuous, more artistic activities, since the city council converted it into the priviledged centre of exhibitions and other cultural events. This is Oporto undergoing renewal without denying its past to which belong broad and ancient spaces such as this square, of black stone cut in the old manner, side by side with more innovative action designed to cater for new movements and the latest ideas.

The lodges where Port wine is aged in enormous barrels.

The "barcos rabelos" used for the transport
of the famous wine.

BARCOS RABELOS, LODGES AND PORT WINE

Renowned world-wide, Port is an old wine with virtues enhanced by glory and a generous portion of popular lore. Although it bears the city's name, the wine is not produced here but comes, in fact, from the steep, terraced hillsides of the interior, near **Régua** and all along the banks where the vineyards rise almost to the heavens in tiers reposing in the sun.

Certainly the lodges are located in the city, but to the west. It is here that the huge number of barrels of the different brand names have always been stored, barrels containing sacred preparations going by the most diverse names and assuming the most varied hues. Transportation downstream was undertaken in *barcos rabelos*, vessels of shallow keel with two foreward oars and central sail for use on the upstream journey, made necessary by the wind patterns in the Douro valley. The barrels, meanwhile, were stacked in the centre of the vessel in superimposed rows down the vessel's length. More modern practises have, however, put an end to this tradition. There is no experience to compare with that of going to the **Solar do Vinho do Porto**, to contemplate the Douro with a glass of glowing port wine in your hand.

Panoramic view of the town of Amarante, and internal court-yard of the Church of São Gonçalo.

Vila Real: Praça do Camões and the manor house of Solar de Mateus.

AMARANTE

This entire area is astonishing. Anybody coming here with the intention of seeing everything in a few days will not find time hanging on their hands. The surrounding country is composed of ranges of hills, fed by water courses meandering discreetly between banks of lush vegetation, boasting pines and eucaliptus of ever-changing green, as is each plot of land which the local people have sub-divided over the years to the proportions of veritable pocket handkerchiefs. Colours hover in the air, waterfalls reflect the blue of the sky and the white of the clouds, the granite of the bridges, monastries, churches and mansions, while the houses of Amarante crouch over the river as though intent on observing every detail of its passage or ascertaining whether the water is really moving despite its silence. Mysteries which the romanesque **São Gonçalo bridge**, with its perfect arch, could doubtless reveal. The streets are narrow and range the humblest dwelling side by side with the gravity of the **churches of São Gonçalo, São Pedro** and **São Domingos**. Gastronomically, the region rewards the visitor with a *pão-de-ló de Margaride* (delicate sponge cake), a range of sweetmeats going back through the timeless pages of

Lamego: the pilgrimage church of Nossa Senhora de Remédios.

Chaves: the Parish Church opposite the pillory; below, the Roman bridge.

history, *papos-de-anjo* (angel craw), *toucinho do céu* (heaven's bacon). A trip through the area around Amarante is strongly recommended: **Felgueiras** with its fine laces, white and elegant, **Gatão** justly proud of its **Igreja Matriz** (parish church), the **Mosteiro de São Salvador** in **Travanca**, the romanesque church of **Vizela**. Not to be omitted is the city of **Vila Real** and, or course, **Mateus**, a borough of that city. Its toponymy is characterized by the world-famous rosé wine, bearing a view of the **Solar de Mateus** (manor house) on its label. The manor house itself is one of the most beautiful in the country, with every stone attesting in unparalleled splendour to the richness of Portuguese baroque. Everywhere, the works of man blending perfectly with their surroundings.

LAMEGO

In this region the villages seem to hide from each other, using the hillsides and copses to conceal their whereabouts, living resigned in their isolation. **Lamego** is an ancient city, situated between the roads linking inland Portugal with the lands beyond the Rio Douro, the Spanish plains with the Portuguese coast.

The town today is yet imbued with an atmosphere of the past, its castle riding proud on the highest hill on which the medieval homes were built, known as the **Bairro de Almacave**. From the square rises a mighty and richly decorated stair towards the **Pátio dos Reis**, leading the visitor to the the pilgrimage church or **Santuário de Nossa Senhora dos Remédios**.

CHAVES

It is said that the valley was once the mouth of a volcano and, in fact, the famous spas here would seem to support this theory. The city, situated but a few kilometres distant from the Spanish border, was founded in 104 AD under the original name of **Aquae Flaviae** in homage both to the Roman emperor and to the excellence of the sulphuric waters which bubble permanently from the ground at a regular temperature of 73 degrees centigrade. The emperor's name is still to be seen engraved on the two cylindrical pillars supporting either end of the Roman bridge with its series of arches linking the centre of the city with the Madalena district.

The **Rua Santo António** is without a doubt the commercial backbone of Chaves, rivalling another, less linear street which is, paradoxically, named **Rua Direita**

Bragança surrounded by its ancient walls.

Pinhão: an ''azulejo'' which decorates one of
the outer walls of the station.

(Straight Street) which is more residential in nature with
pretty, wooden balconies overhanging the pavements. In
the centre, the **Largo das Freiras** and the **Jardim do
Bacalhau** display flower-decked nooks in permanent
competition with the vast area of the **Jardim Público**
(park) and flower beds surrounding the **Torre de Mena-
gem**, the keep that King Dinis had built and which now
houses the **Museu Militar** (Military Museum). The view
from the top of the tower is magnificent indeed: close by,
the Romanesque façade of the **Igreja Matriz** (parish
church) and the pillory, in the middle ground, the tranquil waters of the Rio Tâmega, the forts of São Francisco
and São Neutel. Finally, in the distance, the fertile plain
and the surrounding mountains beyond which lie countless interesting places: **the hot springs** of Vidago and
Pedras Salgadas, the **Monforte Castle**, the **Valpaços Igreja de Santo Estevão**, dozens of villages which seem to
have grown out of the very ground over hundreds of
years.

In **Pinhão**, which lies right on the waters of the Rio
Douro from where it surveys the surrounding vineyards,
the visitors might like to include a visit to the station
building in their itinerary. The outside walls are lined
with tiles depicting scenes from the wine industry, thus
providing a valuable ethnographical study of the whole
subject of wine-making.

BRAGANÇA

The countryside is scattered with olive trees, vines, almond trees, chestnuts, pine, fruit trees of every imaginable variety which manage to survive the hot summers and harsh winters. The city is built on a hilltop, gazing complacently down upon those who dare not venture so far, distant as it is from the sea and the major urban centres, its isolation enhanced by the precariousness of the public roads. Aloft, **the castle**, in an excellent state of preservation, encloses within its walls the entire medieval city and a proud keep. Opposite the fort, the *Domus Municipalis*, (Town Hall) built on top of a cistern, meeting place of local scholars. Beyond the **Casa do Arco** is to be found the **Museu do Abade de Baçal**, to which two storeys have been added, together with extensions in the gardens of the former **Paço dos Bispos** (Bishops' Palace), room after room of noteworthy works of art, Roman sculptures, renaissance furniture, china and portraits. A climb up **São Bartolomeu** leaves the city far behind, far enough to make it possible to view the whole, a sight that will remain lastingly imprinted on the visitor's memory.

Bragança: a view of the centre of the city.

The vineyards of the valley of Rio Douro.

OVAR

Situated on the northern-most branch of the Ria de Aveiro, Ovar now concentrates on industry, replacing the traditional professions of the local people such as fishing, coastal trade, boat building, work in the salt pans beneath the scorching sun. The sole reminder of those days are a few tile-faced buildings. Ovar is also known for its Carnival when the streets are filled with the lively floats.

AVEIRO

Situated on the *Ria* (lagoon), not far from the Atlantic coast, Aveiro is one of the cities of Portugal to have made most economic progress, at the cost however of age-old activities which strongly influenced the place and even now account for much of what a visitor will encounter. Aveiro has borne a number of different names in its time, relating to its physical characteristics or to local professional activities which left their mark. Aveiro is, for instance, the Venice of Portugal, on account of its numerous canals bearing the elegant *barcos moliceiros*, the traditional seaweed transporting boats of the lagoon, with their proud upward-sweeping prow and multicolour decoration. It is also the Aquatic City, water being its preponderant element. It is likewise known as the Salt Factory since from here comes the element that will later

Characteristic boats on the Ria de Aveiro.

season the cuisine not only of Portugal but also, until a few years ago, of the countries of Northern Europe who imported this culinary ingredient. Aveiro has been given yet another name, City of Tiles, in homage to the countless buildings with façades of this traditional decorative material, such as, for instance, the **Igreja da Misericórdia**, the doorway of which is, in addition, a perfect example of the late Renaissance period.

The Church of Santa Maria de Valega, on the outskirts of Ovar.

Aveiro: the square with the Church of the Misericórdia and the Town Council Palace.

Typical houses on the Costa Nova.

On the following pages: the exsiccation of cod-fish, the salt-works and the port and the beach of Figueira da Foz.

FIGUEIRA DA FOZ

This city lies in a privileged location indeed: standing beside the estuary of the Rio Mondego, it enjoys an immense beach christened Praia da Claridade (Beach of Brightness) on account of the intense sunlight reflected all along the endless stretch of sand. Close by lies the Serra da Boa Viagem, for upland range offering the city natural protection from the strong north winds and a magnificent view over the entire region with the infinite ocean on the one hand and the fertile, moist farming land of the Mondego divided into squares of every shade of green on the other. And not so far beyond, to the east, the eyes may behold the elegant silhouette of the **Castelo de Montemor-o-Velho** on days when the sun shines and the air is clear, as indeed is generally the case.

And, on the gastronomic front, a stay here would not be complete without sampling at least some of the endless local fish-based dishes — whether salt or fresh water — and the local sweetmeats: *brisas* (breezes) and *pastéis da Figueira* (Figueria cakes), *leite-creme* (milk-creme), *penhascos de amêndoa* (almond crags), *argolas de açúcar* (sugar rings), arch-rivals of the sweetmeats of neighbouring **Tentúgal**, a short distance inland. All these treats are to be found in abundance during any of the festivities for which this city serves as stage: *Santos Populares* in June, in honour of São João, São Pedro and Santo António (St John, St Peter and St Anthony). These are celebrations of a popular nature held on a regular basis and which are very different from the exclusive atmosphere of the city's casino required of anybody desiring to try their luck at the roulette wheel.

The Hotel do Buçaco.

Coimbra: general view and the internal court-yard
of the Monastery Santa Clara-a-Nova.

COIMBRA

They call this the students' city, on account of its ancient university, in fact one of the oldest in Europe. But to confine the description of Coimbra to these terms is to unjustly limit it to what is only one, albeit fascinating but certainly not the most important, of its facets. It is a city built to the measure of its inhabitants, neither over-large nor excessively small, neither cosmopolitan nor provincial. It is a city of a size which allows the local people to meet down on Rua Ferreira Borges or Rua da Sofia while about their daily shopping. The stall-holders in the Mercado Central know the regular customers and the people sitting in the cafes have an air of being very much at home. Nobody is in any particular hurry, the minutes are meant to be spent one at a time.

The highest part of the city is occupied by the medieval town which barely offers room for the roads carrying the inhabitants about their daily business. This is where the **Sé Velha** (old Cathedral) is situated, a church built in the true romanesque style in the times of the battles against the Moors and, for this reason, bearing battlements of

which any war-intended construction would be proud. Another large place of worship, the **Sé Nova** (new Cathedral) is one of the buildings best representing the Coimbra version of the baroque style of the XVII century. The university is also situated in this upper section, consisting of new buildings in the Estado Novo style, sited beside the old school, with its **João V library** and court affording fine views over the Rio Mondego, a leisurely waterway which seems to disappear during the torrid summers. That is the time of the year when the locals leave the city behind, heading either for the Algarve or, for those wishing to remain closer to home, installing themselves on the plentiful sands of the **Figueira da Foz** beaches, or sheltering in the hillside shade of the Serra do Buçaco, where the ornate tower of the Hotel do Buçaco — in the Manueline style — peeps over the tree tops.

The students, for their part, with the annual Queima das Fitas (ribbon burning) ceremony over and in possession of their exam results, leave Coimbra to return only a few months later.

It seems that, during these quiet months, the city recuperates its strength, ready to welcome back the townsfolk

when they return to fill the streets once more with customary bustle. The gardens are at their peak: the Sereia plunges down the hillside, its pathways shaded by trees and kept cool by the many discreetly murmuring fountains, the **Botanic Gardens**, luxuriant gathering of species from both tropical and temperate climes; the Choupal, overhanging the Rio Mondego and witness of more than one affair of the heart, the Penedo da Meditação, where verses are concealed between the weeping stands of ivy. On the opposite bank of the river, it seems that the Quinta das Lágrimas to this day observes strict silence for the death of Inês de Castro, the living symbol of one of the most tragic love affairs in the history of Portugal.

The left bank of the river is likewise the site of **Portugal dos Pequenitos** where miniature reproductions of the most typical buildings and monuments of Portugal and her former colonies are grouped in an open-air setting. A little further afield, the visitor may also visit the **Mosteiro de Santa Clara-a-Nova** of irreproachable architectural balance.

Fifteen kilometres down the southbound road, near Condeixa, is **Conimbriga** and its **open museum of Roman ruins**. The most inspiring element among the houses, fountains and ramparts are, undoubtedly, the mosaics that are to be seen.

The Sé Nova and the interior of the University Library.

The Sé Velha and a view of the "Portugal dos Pequenitos", a big garden where there are miniature reproductions of the most typical buildings of Portugal.

Roman ruins of the city of Conimbriga.

VISEU

The old part of the city is gathered harmoniously on a hill topped by the cathedral which, along with the **Museu Grão Vasco**, shares the beautiful, ample space of one of the prettiest squares in Portugal.

Every nook in Viseu bears witness to days long past, sixteenth century doors and windows, churches with magnificent altars alternating with houses displaying windows of utmost simplicity or meticulously carved in the Manueline style, tiles testifying to the splendour of an age of artistic splendour. The paintings by Vasco Fernandes in the Grão Vasco Museum are sure proof of this. But it is not only the late medieval period that has left its mark. The XVII and XVIII centuries were to produce chapels, palaces and fountains in high baroque style, innumerable architectural elements making Viseu a place in which the past envelops us. The air is redolent of resin and pine, exuded by the woods and forests around this city composed of irregular rows of houses separated by labyrinthine streets along which the local inhabitants stroll in leisurely fashion, from Rossio to the Rua Direita, be it a normal day or amid the bustle of the Tuesday market to which the entire city turns out.

Viseu: the Sé and a detail of the internal court-yard of Grão Vasco Museum.

GUARDA

The city is dominated by the mighty **Sé** (cathedral), construction of which was begun in about 1390, though completed only two centuries later. Its lines, their weight emphasized by the starkness of the stone, is relieved somewhat by the pinnacles and trefoils crowning the whole. Inside may be seen an immense medieval altarpiece composed of over a hundred figures depicting the life of Christ, from birth to cruxifiction.

Scattered throughout the city are a number of churches bearing witness to the passing of time and the evolution of styles through the ages. Most notable of these are the **churches of São Vicente** and **Misericórdia**, both flanked by belfries and with interiors decorated in purest baroque style with altars and pillars lending a magnificent dignity. Strolling through its streets, the visitor will encounter charming examples of lay architecture, such as the XVIII century drinking fountain beside the hospital or the renaissance window sculpted in harsh granite which adorns the outer wall of a house in Rua Direita. A city with a history receding far into the past but, simultaneously, present on every corner. An inland township gaz-

Guarda: the façade and the interior
of the Church of the Misericórdia.

Views of Manteigas and Castelo Rodrigo,
two towns near Guarda.

Two pictures of the gardens of the Paço Episcopal.

D. JOÃO II
O PRINCIPE
PERFEITO

D. DUARTE
O FLOQUENTE

ing over the plain streching beyond the castle walls to beyond the border. Along that same border lie numerous stoutly walled towns and villages rising above a rural landscape, such as the fortified town of **Castelo Rodrigo**. This entire area of Portugal is mountainous, far above sea level. The highest mountains of the country are the Estrela range, Serra da Estrela, rising to an altitude of almost 2000 metres. Close by, the city of **Covilhã** with its industrial tradition in textiles, and the town of **Manteigas** with houses tumbling down the steep valley sides, cold indeed in winter but extremely pleasant in summer. And there is no excuse for leaving this area without sampling the most famous cheese of Portugal, the renowned *queijo da Serra*.

CASTELO BRANCO

This city falls into two markedly different districts. One is the modern section characterized by elongated buildings with different-shaped windows breaking the white expanse of wall. The second is the older district of nar-

An evocative view of the Castelo de Leiria.

row, uneven streets as might be expected in a city which inherits its irregular configuration from the Middle Ages. It is in the latter area that the finest examples of Manueline doorways are to be found. The **Museu da Cidade**, housed in the former **Paço Episcopal** (Bishop's Palace) with its lengths of wall featuring windows crowned by meticulously carved stone, enjoys one of the most important baroque gardens existing in Portugal, with its immaculately clipped hedges enclosing almost pond-like spaces containing stone statues of the successive kings of Portugal.

LEIRIA

The area is covered by pinewoods, stretching as far as the eye can see, vast expanses of intensest green permanently irrigated by numerous water courses. Nothing jars in this landscape, total calm prevails, calm which is an integral part of the region. One hill succeeds another equally gentle. With the exception of course of the **Castelo de Leiria**, rising dauntlessly before the entire city. Construction of

the castle was begun in the time of King Afonso Henriques, on the remains of a Moorish site. During the following eras it was subject to regular improvements and innovations introduced to meet the needs of the moment. The castle and the **Igreja de São Pedro** are the sole examples of medieval buildings to be found in the entire city. But it nonetheless has far-reaching roots, stretching back to times now forgotten, for which reason it contains many other works constructed over time, years and years of history in each stone. A prime example is the **Sé** (cathedral), of ancient construction dating from 1559 with a façade revealing the austerity characteristic of the religious architecture of the Portugal of that day, sober lines containing a less restrained interior. Scattered all over the city, reminders of religious faith punctuate the urban fabric: here the **Igreja da Misericórdia**, there the **Igreja do Espírito Santo**, beyond, the **Santuário** (pilgrimage church) **de Nossa Senhora da Encarnação** and the **Paço Real** (Royal Palace). Places of worship in various styles standing before houses, gardens, parks, statues and balconies; in short, an urban conglomeration standing graciously on the banks of the Rio Liz.

A general view, and some details, of the famous Monastery of Santa Maria da Vitória.

BATALHA

Leaving Leiria on the motorway, the landscape is abruptly interrupted. Without warning, the **Mosteiro de Santa Maria da Vitória** looms unannounced over the motorway. This construction was built on the orders of King João I to commemorate with due pomp and circumstance the victory over the Spaniards in the battle of Aljubarrota by which the Portuguese won a struggle for independence that had dragged on painfully for a number of years.

It can be said that the town of Batalha was born of the monastery. It took centuries to complete construction — being finally declared complete during the reign of King Joao III — despite the fact that certain parts of the monastery had not yet been translated from the drawing board to reality, in particular the **Capelas Imperfeitas** (Unfinished Chapels). King João, who was responsible for the vow made to the Virgin to the effect that a temple would be erected in keeping with the magnitude of the event, lived to see completion only of the front of the Abbey, the **Founder's Chapel** and a minimal part of the cloister. His tomb was placed in a section of later construction, the **Panteão Real** (Royal Pantheon), built during the reign of King Duarte.

The length of time it took to complete the monastery is apparent in the series of artistic styles appearing in the various components of the construction, combining renaissance elements with typically Manueline-inspired features. Hence, this grandiose monument testifies to the various styles of the successive architects supervising the work over the years. For instance, the main doorway was erected under Huguet, while the interior decoration was undertaken in accordance with the teachings of Boitaca, with his markedly Renaissance touch.

The interior of the church is imbued with a mystic atmosphere, regularly spaced pillars supporting a gothic roof terminated in pinnacles of stone tracery, silent aisles along which saints stand in their niches, arched stained glass windows radiate colour as from a magic kaleidoscope. This is particularly true of a window dating from the XVI century depicting Christ's Passion, the nailing to the cross, the cruxification and finally the descent from the cross. The sun vies with the splendid brightness spilling from the many windows set in the dark stone of the walls.

By reason of its monumental wealth and profuse decoration, the **Mosteiro da Batalha** is indisputably one of the finest manifestations of gothic architecture in Portugal.

Pilgrims in the Sanctuary of the Virgin of Fátima.

FÁTIMA

Prior to the religious event that occurred in 1917 in **Cova da Iria** — situated 2 kilometres outside Fátima — these hillsides were frequented only by shepherds and labourers, the fields were divided by dry-stone walls into tiny plots, trees were scant and the main roads were too far away. The visions, later confirmed by the church authorities, changed all this: the faithful started to visit in large numbers, hospitals were built to tend to the sick who came in search of spiritual solace, trade flourished as never before. With the Second World War, Fátima gained an international reputation and religious ceremonies began to be held regularly, while new religious orders settled near the **Basílica**. Construction of the church, of local white limestone, was begun in May 1928 under the sole responsibility of the Dutch architect Van Kricken. Hence, the basilica is the centre of Cova da Iria, linked by colonnades to the two hospitals embracing the huge esplanade where, between May and October of each year, pilgrims from all over the world gather to celebrate the Immaculate Conception. To north and south, shops selling religious souvenirs, museums depicting the events of 1917 and a number of hotels fill the space on either side of the main Rua Francisco Marto, named after one of the three shepherd children who, together with Lúcia and Jacinta, witnessed the religious phenomenon which is yearly commemorated with such devotion.

The beautiful Praça da República in Tomar.

Some pictures of the Convent of Christ.

TOMAR

Yet another city built on a human scale, stone after stone revealing countless years of Portuguese history, a place that deserves to be visited on foot to give the eyes the chance to peruse at leisure the façades of the houses, rows of buildings with churches alternating with shops where the old occupations stubbornly resist extinction, balconies retiring behind grills of intricate wrought iron, corners lit by the morning sun and withdrawing into thick shade with the passing of the hours. A play of light over which the castle has long become accustomed to presiding. This town is pure history, harbouring an ancient cultural heritage which today still continues to be whole-heartedly embraced, as in June of every other year with the Festa dos Tabuleiros.

The urban layout of Tomar is in the form of a cross, each extremity pointing to a cardinal point with the two branches intersecting in Praça da República. The monuments of the city, the artistic heritage of this Templar Capital, were sited in relation to this fulcral point. The four cardinal points also show the way to a like number of convents: the **Convento de Cristo** to the west — the chapterhouse of which contains an extremely fine **window** constituting the most energetic plastic definition of maritime expression to be found in Manueline art — **Convento de Santa Iria** to the east, **Convento da Anunciada** to the north and the **Convento de São Francisco** to the south.

NAZARÉ

A break in the steep cliff face accomodates a beach where fishermen settled long ago. Today, Nazaré continues to be the home of courageous men, a town where the heart of every one of the inhabitants beats in time to the mighty waves breaking on the sandy shore. The townscape is predominantly white, though sudden whims are manifest in different tones. When this occurs, the blue of the sky is reflected in the sun shades lined up on the beach, black grief takes material form in widows' weeds, the green of nature is carried over to the boats drawn up on the beach until the fall of evening summons the fishermen to take to the water. From **Sítio** — which may be ascended by lift — all this is to be seen. And much more besides: the **Ermida da Memória**, a chapel commemorating the miracle worked by Nossa Senhora da Nazaré in saving a horseman from plunging over the cliff edge as he pursued a stag. Also the coastline, interrupted now and again by a town or village, and the open sea extending to a distant horizon gently dividing sky and ocean. Not far away is the shell-shaped bay of **São Martinho do Porto**, where the turbulent ocean finds temporary calm.

Aerial view of the beach of Nazaré.

The Roman aqueduct near Tomar.

74

ALCOBAÇA

This town continues to stand as though virtually immune to unbridled progress, a collection of buildings resting placidly on the banks of the Rio Alcoa and the Rio Baça, the names of which seem to have magically mingled to give this town its name.

The settlement is dominated by the **Mosteiro**, the **Real Abadia de Santa Maria de Alcobaça**, construction of which was initiated in 1178 under the supervision of the superiors of the Cistercian Order though it later had a series of extensions added. The tombs of Inês de Castro and King Pedro I stand one on either side of the transept, both magnificent XIV century works of their kind, demonstrating particularly fine medieval carving.

Despite the sheer size of the building — with its lofty main front and magnificent central cloister dedicated to King Dinis — the interior does not reflect the exterior grandeur. On the contrary, the decoration is simple and even austere in strict accordance with the rules of the Cistercian monks.

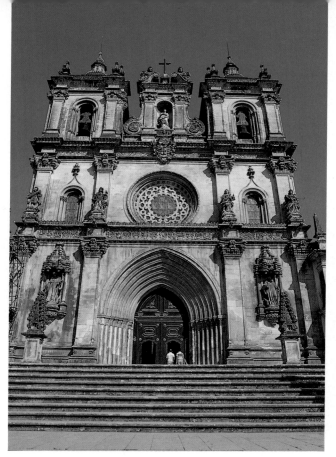

The façade of the Monastery of Santa Maria and the tomb of king Pedro I.

A view of the Medieval castle at Óbidos that dominates the city.

The Gothic style pillory and in the background, the church of Santa Maria with its Renaissance portal.

ÓBIDOS

For centuries the ancient city of **Óbidos** was a port – at least until the navigable river that linked it to the sea diminished during the sixteenth century. What has remained intact however, is its traditional name as the "Wedding City." This is linked to a specific historic event. In 1282 the king Dinis gave the then small hamlet of Óbidos to his bride Isabella as a wedding present, all the Portuguese kings who followed would take their new brides to this increasingly flourishing town immediately after the wedding. Today Óbidos is a charming town where the whitewashed houses, with colorful, flower-filled balconies crowd the narrow cobblestoned streets.

The city gate is covered with 18th century azulejos with the reliquary of Nossa Senhora da Piedade.

Houses trimmed in blue stand at Óbidos.

The city is still protected by its old fortified walls that have four gates: **Porta do Vale** on the east, **Porta da Cerca** and **Porta do Telhal** on the west and **Porta da Vila** with its splendid *azulejos* decorations on the north. It is this last gate that leads into the heart of the city via the Rua Diretta, "the straight street", the city's main artery that goes to piazza where the **Igreja de Santa Maria** stands. This church, that is famous for its splendid seventeenth century *azulejos* is where the future king Alfonso V still a child was married to his cousin Isabella in 1441. The church also has a beautiful painted wooden ceiling, an altar piece (*The Mystic Marriage of St. Catherine*) by Josefa de Óbidos, a famous Spanish artist who lived here in the 17th cen-

The medieval city of Óbidos and its walls.

A picture of the grottos of Alvados.

tury and is buried in the just as beautiful **Igreja de Sao Pedro**.

Óbidos, proud of being her second home, has dedicated much space in the **Museu Municipal** to her works. However, anyone who reaches the city via the lush countryside with its famous vineyards and delightful windmills, will be struck by the majestic turreted **castle** that dominates from on high and seems to protect the little white houses.

Built in the XII century after the city was taken from the Moors – perhaps over an existing defensive bulwark, it was rebuilt in the following century by order of king Dionigi and perfectly anchored to the perimeter of the city walls. It is certainly worth seeing. The bastions and the guards' path along the walls, afford a splendid view of the city and we can fully

The Castle of Almourol.

Windmills in the country-side near Peniche.

admire the skill with which the old Medieval buildings blend with the later sixteenth-seventeenth century structures that were erected during the city's greatest period of "modern" splendor.

The result is a fascinating urban complex that has achieved a perfect harmony of extremely different architectural styles and typologies.

ALMOUROL
ALVADOS

The area is divided into small, tranquil villages, fresh pinewoods and extensive fertile river flats: from **Dornes**, the visitor might like to travel to **Ferreira do Zêzere** and on to Tomar by way of the fascinating caves at **Alvados**. The greatest river of the Iberian Peninsula, the Tagus, crosses this entire area, feeding hill side and valley with

Cabo Carvoeiro.

The rocky Berlengas Islands.

an inexhaustible, life-giving stream. Just before reaching the area of the *lezíria*, the fertile river flats, an islet is to be seen rising from the river, somewhere between **Vila Nova da Barquinha** and **Constância**, and on this islet the **Castelo de Almourol** was erected by the followers of Gualdim Pais, master of the Order of the Templars of the day. The archeological finds made during the successive restorations of the fortress have further enhanced the mystery surrounding its walls, tales passed by word of mouth down through the generations telling of knights in love with noble ladies, sad but kindly giants, grim duels fought for the love of one or another, deeds of long long ago on the banks of a silent river.

CABO CARVOEIRO BERLENGAS

The coastline today is a continuous line of rocky drops plunging sheer into the sea, cliffs alternating with small coves, tiny clusters of houses separated from the waters of the Atlantic by tiny beaches with a few cultivated fields tormented continually by the wind. The coast extends from north to south. However, this was not always the case. In fact, in the XV century, the area currently occupied by **Peniche** and **Cabo Carvoeiro** was an island, a tiny head of land which was gradually joined to the mainland by the accumulation of stone and sand. And **Atouguia da Baleia**, for example, formerly a harbour, now lies peacefully surrounded by farmland in the **Vale de Ferrel**. The former island of Peniche, for its part, is nowadays a major fishing centre, a charming town with pretty churches such as that of **Nossa Senhora da Ajuda** and **Nossa Senhora da Conceição** who vies for the devotion of the local inhabitants with the patron **Nossa Senhora dos Remédios** in whose honour one of the region's most solemn processions takes place every 19 October.

The town was first fortified in the early XVI century and periodically strengthened during succeeding centuries with further walls. Thus the **Forte da Cabana**, the **Forte da Luz**, the **Forte da Consolação** and the **Forte de São João Baptista** came into being, the latter situated on the adjoining archipelago, a series of tiny islands named **Berlengas, Forcadas and Farilhões**, aged witnesses of the change undergone by the Portuguese coastline over the centuries. If you visit these tiny fragments of land emerging from the immensity of the ocean, keep your eyes open for the immense variety of species of migratory birds which periodically visit these islands.

Alpiarça: the "Casa dos Patudos".　　　　　　　　*An aerial view of Santarém and - below - the Sé.*

SANTARÉM

This city, an outspread sheet of white houses, stretches over raised ground from where it stares fixedly at the river. The details of its founding are lost in the mists of time, though one thing is certain: it has always been a city of importance within the Iberian Peninsula, both as a prime position from the geo-strategic point of view and as place of passage between north and south, east and west. It was once a Roman city and was for many years called Scallabis, even after it was conquered by the Moors. However, after possessing the city for many years, the Arabs eventually started to call this city Sant' Arein, in denunciation of the fervent worship of the local Santa Iria. Many vestiges remain of the Moorish period, the lay-out of the streets, the nature of the houses of the

old centre, marks of antiquity which make this city an open air museum.

The visitor should head their list of places to visit with the **Largo do Seminário**, the **Largo Central** and the **Portas do Sol**, the nineteenth century gardens serving as a magnificent balcony overlooking the Tagus. Santarém may be seen in its entirety from the top of the **Torre das Cabeças**, the unusual clock tower. From here, the eyes may feast upon ample windows, church towers, tile-clad façades, narrow streets crouching out of reach of the scorching sun, luxuriant trees lending a touch of freshness to this city lying beneath an intensely blue sky. The fertile river flats, the *lezíria*, furrowed their entire length to allow the river to flow through, is dotted with small villages living in the shadow of the castle, the olive groves and the parish church. In **Alpiarça**, the visitor should be sure to see the **Casa dos Patudos**, a fine country residence built between 1905 and 1909 and revealing an unusual architectural style in the design of its galleries.

83

MAFRA

This town, set in a hollow between the hills, is totally dominated by the **convent**, construction of which was begun in 1717 and completed only eighteen years later. The decision to undertake such a vast project was the product of a vow made by King João V to the effect that he would build such a monument in Mafra if his wife, Maria Ana of Austria, gave him a son. Joy at the child's birth thus contributed to the grandiosity of the project: 220 metre façade, stone and marble in quantities never before conceived, statues carved in Italy which proved extremely laborious to transport to their destination intact, enormous bells and a number of foreign master-builders to supervise the work.

This mighty monument certainly merits a visit: 40,000 square metres occupied by buildings, cloisters, huge gardens and a number of courtyards, all designed and constructed in accordance with ideas from abroad, ranging from ornate Austrian baroque and Italian sensitivity to the sumptuousness of Palace of Versailles. Of course, the gold which was just beginning to arrive from Brazil lent additional fervour to the artistic and devote impulses of the Portuguese monarchs.

Two views of the internal court-yard of the Convent of Mafra.

LISBON

Lisbon, so legend has it, was founded by Ulysses, traveller who named the place Olisipo. Later, in 1200 BC, came the Phoenicians who, having no records at their disposal, christened this coast with the new name Alis Ubbo for the convenience of anybody who might be interested. With the arrival of the Romans, the town came to be called Felicitas Julia, now a more important place but retaining as ever the light and appearance lent it by the landscape. As a stronghold, the city was coveted by the Moors who subsequently conquered and called it Al-Ushbuna, a name the Christians continued to use when the city was won back from the Arabs in 1147. Every stone tells a story, of how the city survived major and alarming upheavals, the wars for royal ascendency, the struggle against Castile, the devastating earthquake of 1755, the 1988 fire engraved on memory as a combination of flame and tears shed over the tragic loss of a unique and irreplaceable district. But man does not dwell on sadness alone, and much less do cities. There were times of glory and laughter, of collective euphoria and shared wealth, smiles exchanged between strangers. Such a time was when the ships returned from previously uncharted shores, when independence was won back, when in April 1974 the streets were strewn with red carnations, replacing the red of the blood shed in the colonial wars in Africa.

So many tales the city might tell if it could but express itself aloud. Nonetheless, the city communicates what it feels in other ways. And so clearly that none can fail to understand. The sadnesses and flights of fancy confessed in *fado* song, with the Madragoa, Alfama and Bairro Alto quarters of the city as confidantes of such bitter pain and amusing incidents. There are gardens of palms, acacias and jacarandas where lovers' tiffs are healed by an embrace. Things which are part of life and which the people of Lisbon learned long ago to accept. Perhaps because they know that every day is different, that sooner or later there is always cause for celebration, when eyes shine with emotion. And when the city festivities take the people out into the streets, when the Christmas lights illuminate the winter nights, when the picturesque Bairro Alto fills with people, then the restaurants, cafes and bars witness the looks of complicity furtively exchanged. And when the night is over, the sun rising over the city is discreet in its task of wakening the people and dwellings, gentle rays of exploration before beaming down upon all below the full force of its heat. Then the local people retire to the parks or the cool of cafe interiors, and it would seem that there is not enough shade for so many people. And at dusk the entire city takes on a new colouring, apparent only to the attentive eye. This is when the castle breaths the sea breeze and mirrors the last drowsy rays of the sun. The avenues echo with hurried steps, cars hoot, calls of newspaper and lottery ticket vendors, smoke of roasting chestnuts.

PRAÇA DO COMÉRCIO

This is where Lisbon originates, maritime city *par excellence* inviting the visitor to ascend the shallow steps from the river to dry land and enter its domains. The Colunas Quay is the front door and the Praça do Comércio the waiting room, as a splendid pink embrace greeting all men of good will. It is a noble spot, a stately entrance way into Lisbon.

In its centre rises the equestrian statue of King José, acclaimed by the trumpets played by the surrounding figures. Wild beasts allude to the fantastic journeys made to Africa and India. In the centre of the northern side of the square is the **arch** leading to Rua Augusta proudly depicting the coronation of Glory surrounded by the greater virtues, Genius and Courage. Present also are Nuno Álvares Pereira, Vasco da Gama, the warrior Viriato and Pombal, figures of olympian dignity watching confidently over the square to which the arches on three sides lend rhythm and lightness.

ROSSIO

This is the hub of Lisbon, the point of convergence of increasingly heavy traffic, people crowding its pavements on their way to a meeting with destiny, fountains gushing water, flower vendors displaying their wares and, adding further movement to the constant flurry, the flocks of pigeons which have long become accustomed to the com-

The Praça do Comércio.

The monument to King José: the arch that leads to the Rua Augusta.

The "Teatro Nacional de Dona Maria II" in the main square of Lisbon and, below, a fountain and the statue of King Pedro IV.

motion. This is Rossio, the main square of Lisbon, modest in the architecture marking its boundaries but always displaying a particular colour and its own brand of cosmopolitan activity.

In the centre, high up on his Hellenic-style pillar, King Pedro IV casts an eye over the down-town area, standing in aristocratic pose with an expression revealing his superiority over the meticulously aligned rooftops and streets of this part of the city rebuilt by Pombal after the great earthquake of 1755. At one end of the square stands the **Teatro Nacional de Dona Maria II**, built in the mid-XIX century and blending admirably with the other buildings surrounding the rest of the square.

On the street taking us up to Praça dos Restauradores, we are confronted by a building in neo-Manueline style, with arched doors and adorned with maritime motifs, a modern reproduction of a style which evolved at the time of the Portuguese discoveries of the XVI century. This is Rossio station, daily point of arrival of all who commute into Lisbon to work.

Sta. Justa lift enables people
to reach the Bairro Alto.

The Convent do Carmo.

CHIADO

It is not so much what we see when we stand in the centre of the Largo do Chiado and look around us that is impressive. It is rather what we feel, at the fact of standing in the very spot where Lisbon dons its bohemian mantle, where after an evening well spent people for a time forget the sacrifices of which they normally complain. It is difficult to decide between the opera at the Teatro de São Carlos and the Brasileira open air cafe, between the excesses of the Bairro Alto and a whimsical shopping spree. The best is perhaps just to stay there, to try and discover the exact nature of its atmosphere, whether romantic or scholarly, whether vagabond or popular. Let Camões decide since he has stood there for so long and always proved accurate in his judgements, an aloof presence in the centre of his square watching that unending spectacle. There are a number of churches in the area and even on

Two more pictures of the ruins of the Convent do Carmo.

Praça da Figueira.

In the two following pages: two views of the Castelo de São Jorge and a narrow street of the Alfama, the most ancient city quarter.

the square there are two directly opposite each other vying for patronage of the faithful. Further up, in Largo da Misericórdia, stands yet another. To one side is the Calçada do Combro, down below the Cais do Sodré and Rua do Carmo, part of which was damaged in the summer 1988 fire. Near the upper exit of the **Sta. Justa Lift** (*Elevador*) — erected in 1901 in the Art Nouveau style — the Convento do Carmo lives on, a disturbing ruin raising its fleshless ogival arches towards the open sky. This is all that remained after the 1755 earthquake mercilessly destroyed the buildings on this hill. Further along is the Miradouro de São Pedro de Alcântara, a terrace with a captivating view over Lisbon. All around there are discoveries to be made, streets that have not been given the attention they deserve, shop windows over which to dream. So very many things. The most advisable course might be to revive body and soul with a glass of vintage port in the Solar do Vinho do Porto which is right there, on the spot, near the yellow trams carrying people up and down the steep hill, obligingly shunting backwards and forwards in unending ascents and descents.

PRAÇA DA FIGUEIRA
CASTELO DE SÃO JORGE
ALFAMA

This is the square where the great Lisbon market was held and, though nothing now remains of the building, the tradition at least lives on of meeting here on nights of celebration, such as the feast of Santo António (St Anthony) when the aroma of the grilled sardines *de rigeur* mingle in the air with that of the traditional potted basil. Today the square has in its centre an equestrian statue of King João I and takes pride in being one of the best-positioned spots from which to observe the battlement-crowned hill rising above it.

These are the fortifications of the **Castelo de São Jorge**, a rugged construction won by King Afonso Henriques from the Moors and today a pleasant park, with peacocks and other fowl offsetting the aggression dictating the original construction of the fortress. This is the best site from which to look over Lisbon, with a view over the river from Mar da Palha right down to the estuary, the

91

opposite bank with its smoking industrial chimneys and the cranes of the shipbuilding yards. To the north, you can see the newer avenues with their high rise buildings. On the near-by hillsides, the towers of the magnificent **Igreja de São Vicente de Fora** and of the **Panteão Nacional** (pantheon), and the picturesque Bairro Alto quarter in which the nightlife of Lisbon is concentrated. Returning to the more low-lying areas, your steps follow narrow streets, buildings of only a few floors in height with roofs almost touching across the streets, courtyards, stairways and old cafes, tiny squares giving this close urban maze room to breath. This area combines the quarters of Alfama, Graça and Mouraria, where collective memory may return to the very birth of the Portuguese nation.

SÉ CATEDRAL
IGREJA DA MADRE DE DEUS

If proof were required of the antiquity of Lisbon, then the Sé would certainly bear witness to the truth. Raised on a site already occupied by other creeds — as practised by Romans, Visigoths and Moors — the church was elevated to the category of Episcopal See by the first Portuguese monarch, King Afonso Henriques. The design of the building adheres to the style typical of the XII century: seemingly austere façade, two belfries complete with battlements in testimony of the tribulations of the Christian reconquest underway at that time.

The solid mass of this place of worship dominates the surrounding area, stone upon stone challenging the passing of the centuries. It is not surprising that the surrounding buildings bow at its feet, in deserved deference to such advanced age and mark of gratitude for its determination in keeping alive an unchanging faith dating from antiquity. The three aisles within are illuminated by the light filtering through the brilliant stained glass rose window. The **Baptistry**, surrounded by tiles and standing beneath a dome, served at the baptism of Saint Anthony of Lisbon whose statue stands outside, in a pose revealing sympathy for the prayers of the faithful, indifferent to the relatively modern noise of the trams which even today continue to be widely-used means of transport playing a lively part in the doings of the capital.

On lower ground, at river level, stands the Igreja da Madre de Deus, comprising part of a convent founded in 1509. The interior was renovated in the XVII and XVIII centuries, producing extremely tasteful combinations of style. We see the product here of the ancient art of gilded carving combining happily with religious painting and tiles, a vast selection of which are on display **in the museum** that has been created in the convent cloisters.

The Cathedral.

The entrance to the Church da Madre de Deus.

Two views of the interior.

A fine picture of the Parque Eduardo VII.

The statue of Marquês de Pombal, in the centre of the square dedicated to him.

AVENIDA DA LIBERDADE

The main road artery linking Praça dos Restauradores with **Parque Eduardo VII** is Avenida da Liberdade which was originally considered excessively broad and now barely accomodates so many cars and buses. However, this continual movement in no way detracts from the beauty of this formerly pedestrian mall. It is still possible to walk the distance between Praça dos Restauradores — in its centre an obelisque commemorating independence won from Spain in 1640 — and the Marquês de Pombal roundabout, in the tropical leafy shade of palm trees, be-

The interior of the Museum dos Coches.

side the cool of waterfalls, the ground decorated with Portuguese paving of small black cubes of stone skillfully arranged in a white background.

The Praça do Marquês de Pombal is the hub by which all those travelling from one extreme of the city to the other must pass. In its centre, with a lion as escort, the Marquis watches over modern-day Lisbon. Behind him is the green of Parque Eduardo VII — with its geographically pruned hedges ascending to the crown of the hill — and the Estufa Fria (*greenhouse*) nurturing countless species of tropical flora beneath its fragile roof. The view from this height embraces the entire down-town area and even a blue sliver of the Tagus.

MUSEU DOS COCHES (COACH MUSEUM)
MUSEU DOS AZULEJOS (TILE MUSEUM)

It may be useful to draw attention to the museums which, among all those in Lisbon, contain collections of an originality and wealth meriting a more leisurely visit. This is certainly true of the **Coach Museum** (*Museu dos Coches*) in Belém (Bethlehem), created in the former Royal Manege, the interior decoration of which reveals a very particular appreciation of the neo-classical style. The museum contains a large number of outstanding old vehicles — many dating from the XVII and XVIII centuries — which originally belonged to the aristocracy, the Royal

family or the Patriarchate. In sheer magnificence, one of the most outstanding is the coach in which some of the Marquês de Fonte's ambassadors travelled to Rome to render homage to Pope Clement XI, in 1716.

At the opposite end of the city, certain areas of the **Convento da Madre de Deus** house an extremely valuable collection of Portuguese tiles. In the **Museu Nacional de Arte Antiga** (National Museum of Art), situated in Rua das Janelas Verdes in the Alcântara quarter, paintings by the Medieval masters — a case in point being the "Panéis de São Vincente de Fora" (polyptych from St Vincent's altar), one of the masterpieces of XV century Portuguese art — vie with Bosch's magnificent work "The temptation of St Anthony". In the **Calouste Gulbenkian Museum**, some 5,000 works trace the history of art from classical antiquity to the dawn of the present century, an impressive succession of works by Rembrandt, Monet, Rubens, Lalique, to name but a few.

Above, the carriage of João VI (1824); centre, the gilded carriage of José I (1765); below, a French gala carriage made for the Royal Family of Portugal about the middle of the eighteenth century.

Museo dos Azulejos: a work of the 16th-17th century.

National Museum of Ancient History:
"Polyptych of St. Vincent",
painted by Nuno Gonçalves
(detail).

"The temptation of St. Anthony"
by Hieronymus Bosch.

Calouste Gulbenkian Museum:
view of one of the rooms.

The curious characteristic façade of the Casa dos Bicos.

CASA DOS BICOS

The Casa dos Bicos continues even today to stand beside the Tagus. It is a XVI century building which was partially destroyed during the mid-XVIII century earthquake and has recently been totally rebuilt, with every care to retain the original style. The façade, which is curiously decorated with pointed stones cut like diamonds looks over Rua da Alfândega and the sunny Campo das Cebolas where the scores of palm trees attest to the southerly nature of this Portuguese city.

The offices of the National Committee for the Commemoration of the Portuguese Discoveries are to be found in this building. The Committee organizes and can provide all the information concerning the commemorative events, to last until the year 2000, related to the Voyages of Discovery accomplished by the Portuguese 500 years ago.

Monastery dos Jerónimos: the exterior and the nave of the Church.

MOSTEIRO DOS JERÓNIMOS (HIERONYMITE MONASTERY) TORRE DE BELÉM (BELÉM TOWER)

It was from these very banks that the caravels departed for unknown destinations. But, before reaching such foreign shores, life was pure adventure, days at sea trying to quell fear, mile after mile of salt sea concealing the unknown of its depths and furthest reaches. Those were days when the immensities of the ocean were as wells of secrets upon which only the most courageous dared to even surmise and only the very determined to venture. Their journey would be long, to places they hoped would be fascinating and brimming with wealth but about which they knew nothing for certain. Men struggling year after year against harsh and inhospitable nature, fragile vessels taking on the fury of the elements, sailors believing in the possibility of a better life, routes followed to who knew for sure where.

Belém's monuments tell of all of this and more while the waters of the river, approaching the estuary, whisper to the sand tales of days gone by. The Mosteiro dos Jerónimos, rearing in aloof whiteness, dominates the area, with its Manueline façade rising to its dome in intertwined marine motifs carved into the stone.

Inside is a fine church, three aisles of identical height supported with effortless strength by tall, slim columns. The **Sala do Capítulo** (Chapterhouse) contains the tomb of the writer Alexandre Herculano, while the church harbours those of Camões and Vasco da Gama. The square cloister is two floors high and the carvings adorning its numerous arches lend the whole an incomparable elegance. The magnificent front doorway opens the way to visitors and worshippers between statues, figures drawn from the seafaring art and sculpted artistic effects enhancing the majesty of the monument, built on the orders of King Manuel who consecrated it in the memory of the discovery of the sea route to India. The Monastry is, without a doubt, the most impressive relic of Portugal's maritime exploits and also the most representative work of Manueline architecture.

Lying before it, the expanse of gardens leading to the wind rose and the **Padrão dos Descobrimentos** (Monument to the Discoveries) seems expressly designed to ensure the Mosteiro dos Jerónimos an unhindered view of the Tagus. Close at hand stands the Torre de Belém, the former lookout point over the river entrance, advance bastion protecting the city from undesirables and counting the ships leaving for and returning from new shores carrying fine, exotic goods, revolutionary customs and ways of doing things. When originally built, in 1515, the tower stood further from the water. Now, however, it has the appearance of a ship prevented only by its weight from sailing off downriver towards the open sea. It is strikingly elegant, with its Manueline motifs, discreet balconies and rows of arches. It is the decorative elements of the tower which lend this monument its rare beauty and proportions. An outside wall bears the first attempt to sculpt an African animal, the rhinoceros, demonstrating that these were times of discovery and novelty, pushing back the bounds of knowledge and experience.

Detail of the interior.

PADRÃO DOS DESCOBRIMENTOS
(MONUMENT TO THE DISCOVERIES)

Imposing as a caravel riding the high sea, the Padrão dos Descobrimentos appears to zealously guard the whole of the Belém area, inestimable guardian of the treasures of national heritage built there over the ages.

Built in 1960, the monument stands on a huge wind rose, a homage by the man of today to the man of yesterday. The austerity of its style reveals not only the artistic trend favoured by the Estado Novo (New State) but alludes also to the straight-forwardness of the men taking part in the exploits of the XVI century. Everybody went along, as the statues lining the stone caravel demonstrate: the faithful, the aristocracy, people from the four corners of the land in search of a new direction. And at their head, the Infante Dom Henrique, Henry the Navigator, holding the symbolic caravel which ploughed the ocean waves.

AQUEDUTO DAS ÁGUAS LIVRES
PALÁCIO DE BELÉM

1748 witnessed the inauguration of the great aqueduct, a mammoth undertaking ordered by King João V for the purpose of duly solving the severe shortage of water suffered by the inhabitants of the capital. The total length of the network — with all its distribution channels and branches serving the most underprivileged quarters of the city — amounts to almost 18 kilometres.

Closer to the river, the Palácio de Belém, built by the same king in 1726, rambles through its fine gardens which are not however open to the public in their entirety. The passer-by glimpses only the façade, of simple but perfectly balanced lines, that have witnessed the passage of kings, princes and dignitaries throughout the decades of its existence. This is the official residence of the President of the Republic, containing a number of halls adorned with gilded wooden carvings and pictures by Romantic Portuguese masters. The most noteworthy is the **Sala das Bicas**, adjoining the front entrance, its walls decorated with medallions of jasper and floor decked in chequered marble. In the square before it, a tall-standing **statue of Afonso de Albuquerque**. The pedestal bears bas-reliefs of scenes from the experiences in India of the Viceroy depicted atop the Manueline pillar.

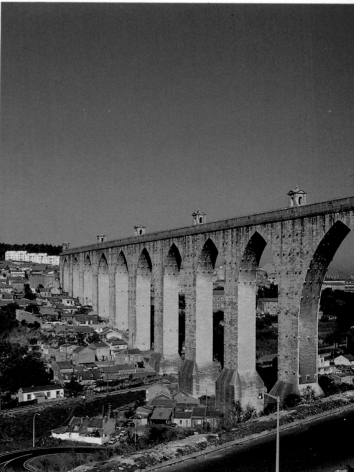

The Tower of Belém, one of Lisbon's most famous buildings.

The Padrão dos Descobrimentos.

The great aqueduct "das Águas Livres".

The Bridge "25th April".

The statue of Christ the King.

25 APRIL BRIDGE
MONUMENT OF CHRIST THE KING

For the people of Lisbon, crossing the river was a time-consuming event requiring careful thought, a matter of days and motive for anxiety. For centuries, the only way to cross to the other bank was in a boat. The ferries came into service relatively recently, but even these required something that is in short supply in the world of today: time. Until, of course, the bridge was opened in 1966 and these considerations could be forgotten. It is an outstanding work of engineering, two pillars anchored to the river bed supporting a carriageway of almost 2,300 metres in length, a suspended structure which, though of massive dimensions, nonetheless gives an impression of lightness. From the other bank, from which one may enjoy a charming view of Lisbon, the **Statue of Christ the King** watches over the safety of all, arms outstretched from the top of a mighty pedestal, seeming to embrace the city opposite and the river at its feet.

FUTURISM IN LISBON

For Portugal in general and Lisbon in particular, 1998 was a highly significant year. From 22 May to 30 September the capital of Portugal played host to **Expo '98**, an event that aroused the whole world's interest and literally changed the face of one of the city's suburbs. The northeast section of Lisbon underwent years of preparation for this, the last big event of the millennium. The result was the modern **Park of the Nations** a lush green setting for the Expo.

Because Lisbon was chosen as the venue since 1998 was the 500th anniversary of the voyage that led the intrepid navigator Vasco da Gama to discover the route to the East Indies via the Cape of Good Hope it was decided to name the new, 12 km long futuristic bridge that was opened in 1997 after him. This spectacular and elegant masterpiece of modern engineering joins Sacavém to Montijo via the Tago north of the Expo area and has made a considerable contribution to alleviating the heavy traffic on Lisbon's other bridge, the Ponte 25 de Abril.

The exhibition's theme was "The Oceans, a patrimony for the future", and Gil was created as the mascot: a stylized wave, personifying water and specifically the ocean. Five pavilions were erected: the **Portuguese Pavilion,** the **Pavilion of the Oceans**, the **Utopia Pavilion**, the **Pavilion of Knowledge of the Seas,** and the **Pavilion of the**

The Vasco da Gama Bridge, a masterpiece of engineering that was opened in 1997. The bridge is named for the famous navigator who discovered the route to the Indies in 1498 and marked the beginning of Portugal's colonial and commercial fortunes.

Future. Two areas: the **International South** and **International North** hosted the individual participating countries. And all around, there was a crown of exhibits, cultural events, concerts, parades and more that involved the entire city for months.

At the conclusion of the Expo, a good part of the spectacular, futuristic structures that had been erected in the Park of the Nations were maintained and have become a part of the city's life and fabric. Furthermore, the entire expo area underwent a complex restructuring within the context of a project aimed at transforming it into a large residential and business center to which government offices and museums would eventually be moved.

The North International Area in particular, was selected as the home of the new **Lisbon Fair**. The Pavilion of the Oceans has been transformed into one of Lisbon's main third millennium attractions.

Designed by the American architect Peter Chermayeff, it stands on the banks of the Tago, and is now home to the **Oceanarium**, the largest aquarium in Europe and the second largest in the world. It comprises five tanks, the largest of which is a cylin-

On these two pages, some of the modern structures that were opened for the great exhibition of 1998.
Opposite page, above, the "multipurpose" pavilion and below, the new railroad station at Comboios.

On this page, two more examples of the futuristic infrastructures that were erected for the Expo and have now become Lisbon's new symbols for the third millennium.

der containing over 6000 cubic meters of water, that is the equivalent of four Olympic sized swimming pools. It holds perfect recreations of the different ocean regions (Atlantic, Pacific, Indian and Arctic) with 25,000 specimens of approximately 300 different species of marine flora and fauna. The various ecosystems have been brilliantly replicated, from coral reefs to the frigid conditions of the Arctic, there is an infinite variety of living creatures that can be viewed up close, and many smaller aquaria where countless fish in sparkling livery swim by. The aim of the exercise is not merely to thrill visitors, but to awaken a deeper respect for the true wealth that the Oceans hold, and a desire to preserve and protect it.

The Pavilion of the Oceans now hosts the Oceanarium the biggest aquarium in Europe and the second largest in the world and one of the "new" Lisbon's greatest visitor attractions.
Above, the exterior of the pavilion and below, a detail of an aquarium where we can see an infinite variety of fish.

Two views of Estoril.

ESTORIL

This coast adjoining Lisbon was the destination of the monied city inhabitants, when the heat of late spring heralded the approach of summer. The palatial homes filled with people who spent their days strolling along **Tamariz beach** and settled themselves commodiously on the sands of **Azarujinha beach**. Gradually, this spot, originally but a fishing village, was transformed into a cosmopolitan centre frequented by royalty, aristocracy and all who aspired to such dignities.

Today, the Casino bears witness to the continuing fashionableness of the resort, the complex overlooking a luxuriant park in which rows of palm trees lend a Mediterranean air to the spot, more restful by far than the tension to which players are subjected by the whims of the wheel or other games of chance. Nothing, however, that cannot be overcome by a stroll along the sea front to **Cascais**.

The lighthouse of Cabo da Roca and a view of Cascais.

CASCAIS

Like many of the places along this stretch of coast extending from **Lisbon** to **Cabo da Roca**, Cascais was no more than a fishing village where the life of the local inhabitants was confined to their daily labour and the task of survival. But times change. The fact that King Carlos frequented these parts during his reign caused Cascais to be raised to the official status of *vila*.

The narrow cobbled streets of olden times are still to be seen in Cascais, winding between houses of severe façade and traditional red tile roofs. Here and there, the odd little square planted with tropical species and palm trees, churches such as that of **Nossa Senhora da Assunção** and of **Nossa Senhora dos Navegantes**. Perched on the rocks lashed by the sea when storms rise, the **Cidadela fort** continues to play an important role in maritime defence. The oasis of this delightful town is the **Parque do Museu dos Condes de Castro Guimarães**, refreshing shade and

The royal palace of Queluz.

ponds in an area incorporating a mansion, a house converted into a museum, as well as a quiet beach and a small zoo. To the west lies **Boca do Inferno** (Devil's Mouth) where the cliff plunges vertically into the ocean. The sea has here dug eerie caves into the rock face which, in rough weather, cause the writhing, volcanic waves to shoot spray high above the over-hanging rocks. This is indeed a beautiful sight when the sun's rays shine through the liquid particles suspended in the air to form hundreds of rainbows.

The visitor, continuing along the coast, will reach **Guincho beach**, an immense expanse of sand like a barrier, its dunes designed to challenge the mighty waves. Further yet, **Cabo da Roca** gazes into the infinite distances of the Atlantic.

The lighthouse sweeps the waters for the safety of passing ships and with its beam of light proudly proclaims that it is the western-most tip of the European continent, where the land ends and the sea begins.

QUELUZ

A little way north of Lisbon lies Queluz which owes its renown entirely to the palace situated on its outskirts, where the buildings make way for open fields. Construction work was begun in 1747, not to be completed until 1786. This palace is an outstanding example of meticulous and refined interior design and is filled with works of art, rooms in which the neo-classical influence is readily apparent and the baroque decoration admires itself shamelessly in the many mirrors adorning the walls. **The gardens** outside stretch for many hectares, green expanses of bushes and clipped hedges, side by side with fountains, ponds and a now empty boating canal lined with sumptuous panels of tiles, scene in days of yore of bucolic punting parties. Nostalgia for the days of grandeur lived by a court which sought, at all costs, to become integrated into the modes of XVIII century Europe, finds its voice in the breeze rustling in the trees.

A view of Sintra from the Moors' castle.

Above, a detail of the Moors' castle that dominates the city and a window of the Palácio Nacional. Below, the palace with its chimneys.

SINTRA

With gardens that enchanted kings and inspired poets, as well as artists through the ages, especially in the nineteenth century, Sintra has long been a favourite. Its name - originally Chintra - comes from Arabic, although its roots have long been forgotten and its legends confused. Among those who have succumbed to its delights are Luís de Camões, Almeida Garrett, Eça de Queiroz, Lord Byron and William Beckford.

In Monserrate, courtiers used to flit in and out of the many shrubs growing in the gardens, and the area retains a magical quality even today.

Suddenly, the landscape juts sharply upwards. It is covered in dense forest, and marks the end of the west coast at Cabo da Roca - the westernmost point of Europe, not counting the Azores. The Sintra hills offer the promise of a journey into times past. In the heart of the town, which is some forty kilometres from Lisbon, there are still traces of the Muslim occupancy of Portugal, with houses with open patios surrounding fountains.

PALÁCIO DA VILA

The National Palace is situated in the main square, in the midst of arcades, ceramic tile decor, Medieval, Renaissance, Baroque and romantic buildings. Little is known of its roots, although there are those who claim that it was inhabited by Arab chiefs. In spite of the many

different views and opinions on the question, the palace was undoubtedly enlarged during the reign of King Dinis. What is also certain is that members of the court spent part of their leisure time there from the time of the Troubadour King. The Aviz dynasty turned the palace into a summer retreat, although keeping the architecture on the same lines.

It was in the palace, then very different from the opulent building of today, that the first expedition to Ceuta was planned. Later, João I received envoys from Philip the Good of Burgundy - amongst whom was the Flemish painter Jan van Eyck - to arrange his marriage with the Infanta Isabel. This is commemorated in one of the rooms: Swans, which were symbols of the house of the groom, were painted on the ceiling, one for each year of the bride's age.

Other ceilings also feature birds such as the **Magpie Room**. Each magpie - also denoting a courtesan in Portuguese - bears the expression "Por Bem" - all for the good - written on it. This was the inept excuse offered by João I when Phillipa of Lancaster caught him kissing one of her ladies-in-waiting. Because of the rumours and intrigue that followed, the king had the ceiling painted with 136 magpies - one for each lady-in-waiting.

The palace's Gothic chimneys are a sign that the court of the early Aviz dynasty spent much of their time there in some splendour. Eye-catching, the chimneys are gigantic cones and can be seen for miles. They must have provided

Above, Palácio da Vila, the Room of the Stags; center and bottom, two fountains in Sintra: one is decorated with multicolored majolicas, the other is adorned with Arab-style tiles.

a more than adequate outlet for the smoke which came from the endless preparation of food in the enormous kitchens.

Afonso V, who died here in 1481, built on to the palace. João II was proclaimed king here, and showed a marked preference for the location, spending many a summer in the royal residence. He too carried out renovation work on the building. However, most of the work was done during the reign of Manuel I between 1505 and 1520. The eastern wing was added and is typical of the art of that time. Twin windows were also added, decorated in luxurious Gothic-naturalist ornament, as well as the rounded arches in the galleries. The **Salão dos Brasões** dates from the same period - 72 coats-of-arms of the nobility at that time are shown. The room's cubic structure and high pyramid-shaped ceiling are typical of the Manueline style. Under the Moorish cornice is a large honeycombed frieze.

The palace houses the largest and most important collection of antique *azulejos* in Portugal. Of note are the **Swan and Magpie Rooms**, which contain rare examples in azul-de-fez, the **Arab Room**, tiled with the chequered Seville wainscots and the Manueline *azulejos* with fleurs-de-lys and sheaves of corn, which decorate the frieze. The beautiful **Gothic chapel** also deserves special mention, with its Islamic ceiling and traces of Gothic paintings.

The palace has been the scene of many events and countless styles have merged here - it was in the palace that the Infanta Maria, sister of João III, had her ladies' court, a place of culture where the ladies spoke Hebrew, Greek and Latin. All this has contributed towards the palace's delightful aura, which can still be felt.

For all that, one of history's most painful episodes is engraved in the floor of a small side room. This was the prison of Afonso VI for the last nine years of his life, where he died in physical and mental agony.

PALÁCIO DA PENA

The Sintra hills can be seen for miles, rising into the sky like a towering fortress, adorned here and there with houses, mansions and other buildings. The Pena Palace sits on the top of one of the peaks, like a crown. What is left of the grey ramparts of the **Moorish Castle** snakes through the green of the forest. The castle was built in the eighth or ninth century by the Arabs, and was taken in 1147 when Afonso Henriques extended the power of the Christians as far as Sintra. The ramparts, which were rebuilt during the reign of Fernando I, have been changed over the years due to restoration work and damage inflicted by the earthquake of 1755. Fernando II also carried out work on the ramparts and some of the towers, and this is what can be seen today. However, the interior still retains some pre-Romanesque remains of a chapel which possibly dates from before the Reconquest.

On the top of the next hill there was a grotto where the Virgin Mary is said to have appeared. A small chapel was built there dedicated to Nossa Senhora da Penha. Priests from the Church of St. Mary of Sintra used to celebrate mass there every Saturday, by order of João I.

In 1493, João II came to the chapel, accompanied by his wife, and spent eleven days here, in fulfilment of a vow. Manuel I was also devoted to the saint. He ordered the cliff to be cut so as to create a small terrace on which he built the Monastery of the Hieronymite Monks, constructed entirely of wood, to replace the tiny church. Work began in 1503. Barely eight years later, the king decided to rebuild with stronger materials. A beautiful building was constructed out of stone. It had a dome, and also contained a chapel, sacristy, bell tower, workshops, cloisters and a dormitory big enough to accommodate 18 monks.

The design of the monastery is sometimes attributed to the Italian architect Giovanni Potassi, although there are those who claim it was Boytac. Manuel I spent an enormous sum on the project. In the chapel, it is still possible to see the royal coats-of-arms, on the ceilings, surrounded by guilloche tracery and the great deeds of the king, illustrated in the *azulejos*. João III and Queen Catarina also showed great devotion to Nossa Senhora da Penha. They installed the Renaissance retable of jasper and alabaster. It is decorated with images and bas-relief, showing scenes from the New Testament and the Passion of Christ. It is said to be by Nicolas de Chanterenne, or Nicolau Romano, and was commissioned for the chapel's high altar in 1532, to give thanks for the birth of the Infante Dom Manuel. On 30 September 1743, lightning destroyed part of the tower, chapel and the sacristy. A few years later, the earthquake of 1755 caused grave damage. In the first quarter of the nineteenth century, the French invasions made their own nefarious contribution to the destruction of the building. The wars between Liberals and Absolutists also helped to destroy it. The coup de grace came in 1834, when religious orders were disbanded, and the monastery was abandoned. Four years later, Fernando II, prince of the house of Saxe-Coburg-Gotha and husband of Maria II, was in love with Portugal and acquired the ruins. He had a fine artistic sense, and was determined to restore the ruins and make it a summer residence. However, influenced by the artistic Baron von Eschwege - who later designed the park together with Wensceslau Cifka - Fernando decided to build a beautiful romantic palace, which would fit in well with what was left of the sixteenth century building.

Construction began in 1840, starting with the road that is still used today to reach Pena Palace. In 1844, work got underway on the building, headed by the Italian Demetrio Cinnatti.

Above, an azulejo *showing the Palácio da Pena.*
Center and bottom, two view of the Palacio that is situated at 500 meters above sea level on the Serra de Sintra. The palace is a compendium of the Gothic, manueline and Moorish styles with Renaissance and Baroque touches that generally blend well with the architecture.

The palace is the embodiment of a romantic ideal, and much more than a simple monument. It is a blend of rare harmony, despite the revivalist potpourri of styles. Built three decades before the castles of Ludwig II of Bavaria, it is the exponent of an age when the dreams of the powerful prevailed. Through one's eyes, one is transported to ancient Egypt, represented by the plant and animal motifs, cymas and columns; on to the Arab countries by way of the minarets and arches - not to mention the interior of some of the rooms - and the Middle East, represented by the statue at the entrance and in the two-storey cloisters, (although they are decorated with ceramic tiles dating from the Hispano-Arabs to the nineteenth century). The Gothic style is present in the chapel and the cloisters, and at the summit of the domes. The Renaissance influence is apparent in motifs such as the pointed tops of the sentry boxes and the aforementioned sixteenth-century retable.

The palace also has countless magical motifs included in its decoration. A good example of this is the Triton Gate, covered in waves of coral and shells, which also supports the earth, as symbolised by the fruit-laden vines.

The irregular layout of the palace, which is in keeping with the exterior, with its magnificent greenery, does not limit itself to the glories of architecture. The interior is also dazzling, and displays Portugal's history together with the world with which it developed. The art of many of the nations Portugal had contact with, such as India and the Far East, as well as Africa and Europe are represented here. The interior contains fine pieces of furniture, china, sculpture, paintings and other treasures. The National Palace of Pena is the sumptuous waking expression of the splendour of a dream.

Three more views of the Palácio da Pena: above the Arab door; center and bottom, the Ballroom and the Arab Room reveal the lavishness of the palace interior.

SETÚBAL

Medieval Setúbal is apparent in the **Convento de Jesus**, containing the **Museu da Cidade** (Municipal Museum) with its fine collection and place of devotion in the hall-church style with three aisles beneath triple columns twisted to form spirals, the walls lined with tiles revealing a marked Islamic influence. One of Setúbal's most representative churches is the **Igreja de Santa Maria da Graça** with its simple façade and generally austere lines, aisles marked by doric style pillars and the interior walls lined in tile panels depicting the life of the Virgin in detail. The visitor will no doubt be surprised by the church in the Praça do Bocage — named after the satirical XIX century poet — the **Igreja de São Julião** which has been rebuilt several times, most extensively in 1513 when its two Manueline doorways were added.

However, Setúbal has more than its cultural wealth to show the visitor. It is pleasant indeed to stroll the winding streets of the old centre, visit the **Castelo de Palmela**, relax over a drink in the open air cafe of a picturesque little square, absorb the local colour and the sounds of this city overlooking the river likewise thronging with the colours of the ships entering and leaving the busy harbour. And, on the opposite bank of the Rio Sado, **Tróia** and its endless kilometres of beaches to be discovered.

The portal of the Church de Jesus and the fishing harbour, seen from above.

119

The Castle of Palmela and the sheer drop of the Serra da Arrábida cliffs to the sea.

Two pictures of the picturesque port of Sesimbra.

ARRÁBIDA
SESIMBRA

This is the region of the Three Castles: those of **Sesimbra, Palmela** and **Setúbal**, situated only a short distance from Lisbon but far removed from its capital city bustle. This is a place of hills sloping down to the clear blue of the sea. A visit might begin with **Cabo Espichel** and its **Igreja de Nossa Senhora do Cabo**, proceeding then towards Setúbal. First however you will reach Sesimbra, with its fine beach and seventeenth century castle, a fishing village which is gradually moving over to tourism. Then the luminous tranquility of Portinho da Arrábida and, above, the remains of the **Franciscan convent**. Landscapes alternating between the arid grey of dry stone and the luxuriance of bounding vegetation, idyllic hidden spots wrapped in the typical scent of the Mediterranean.

The Convent of São Bernardo and the Fountain de 16 Bicas. Below, a general view of Portalegre.

Elvas: the Church of Nossa Senhora da Consolação.

PORTALEGRE

The crown of the hill towering above the fertile fields of the region features numerous towers which appear to overlap when seen from the distance. But this is merely an optical illusion since they do in fact belong to separate constructions, albeit standing in close proximity. In effect, they are all very different. On the one side is the Sé (cathedral) with its white façade and twin, cone-shaped bell towers lending balance to the enormous width of the building. Opposite, the remains of the centuries-old **medieval castle** which was built to coincide with the mid-XII century birth of the nation. The **convento de São Bernardo**, founded in 1518 and displaying tiles from 1739 is situated north of the city. In the centre of one of the cloisters stands the **Fonte de 16 Bicas**, a fountain built entirely of marble. Lying at the feet of these imposing buildings is the city with certain of the houses at some time occupied by members of the nobility or of the monied classes, displaying windows protected by fine works of wrought iron or of profusely decorated Manueline style. A stay in Portalegre is not complete without a visit to each of the **belvederes** (miradouros) of **São Cristóvão, Senhora da Penha and da Serra**.

ELVAS

The Spanish border lies close at hand, a purely human consideration since the landscape pays no heed to such details. Elvas stands alone in the middle of the plain, an amphitheatre-like aggregate huddled on a rise in the land, confined to an area in which the old and narrow streets barely separate the immaculate houses reposing in rows, the sparkling whitewash contrasting with the dazzling hues of thousands of different plants which the local inhabitants assiduously range along the walls of their homes. There is a castle with well-preserved outer walls, in contrast to those surrounding the town which originally had only three accesses: Porta da Esquina, to the west; Porta de Olivença, to the south and Porta de São Vicente, to the east. **The Aqueduto da Amoreira** superimposes row upon row of arches, lending the massive structure an air of surprising lightness.

A visit to the **Forte da Graça** affords a view of the city from afar, dwarfed by the vastness of the fields of corn and other crops stretching into Spain. Elvas lies somewhere in the heart of all this, a luminous town confined by walls, a series of balconies, chimney pots, church towers.

Estremoz: panorama.

Évora: the Roman temple and a general view.

ESTREMOZ

In the manner of numerous towns of the Alentejo plain, Estemoz is surrounded by a wall, betokening a past far from peaceful with every stone yet recalling suffering, battles and blood. This is an elegant town, seeming to move to the rhythmn of the uneven terrain, hills rearing abruptly from the otherwise flat landscape. Looming over the houses is the aloof silhouette of the **Torre das Três Coroas** (Tower of the Three Crowns), its name testifying the the fact that it was built over three reigns: King Sancho II, King Afonso III and King Dinis.

One of the town's sources of wealth is its marble which, in conjunction with the many whitewashed constructions, lends the town a predominantly light colouring. Since the XVI century, it has been a major arts and crafts centre famous for its richly decorated red clays worked into traditional objects as delicate as they are ancient in origin.

ÉVORA

It is not known for sure when Évora was founded, though certain cultural finds, such as the **Roman temple — the temple of Diana —** in the upper part of the city, in the centre of a pretty square with a look out point, indicates considerable antiquity. Although built in complete disregard of the urban context, the numerous monuments of Évora blend admirably into their architectural background, making any stroll through the city a series of trips into the past and returns to the present. The original town is confined to the space jealously guarded by the city walls. Construction beyond the walls is as a continuation of the bright, simple style of the inner area. The narrow streets open onto squares roofed by the blue sky, with different spots in the city serving as sites for several churches: the Sé in Roman-Gothic style was begun in the XIII century, while the **Igreja do Espírito Santo** and the **Igreja da Graça** reveal a marked influence of

The exterior of the Royal Palace "D. Manuel".

The slender arches of the Church of Saõ Francisco.

Details of the Sé: the cloister and the façade.

the Italian mannerism of the mid-millenium. Other points of interest are the **Capela dos Ossos** (chapel of bones), the **Igreja de São Francisco**, the Praça do Giraldo with its harmonious series of arcades, and the oldest section of the city with its meticulously preserved quaintness, around Rua da Alcáçova de Cima.

This is without a doubt one of the most charming of all Portuguese cities, not only on account of the cultural richness apparent at the turn of every corner but also in the dedication with which the authorities have seen to the preservation of this priceless cultural heritage, giving coherence to the delicate choices that have to be made, day by day, between the values of the past and the needs of the present.

Villa Viçosa: the Palace of the Dukes of Bragança.

VILA VIÇOSA

Abruptly the Alentejo plain is cut short by the imposing town of Vila Viçosa which rises unexpectedly out of the vast seemingly endless expanses, its squares and statues replacing vast fields of wheat, with the **Paço Ducal, Palace of the Dukes of Bragança,** facing onto a large square contrasting with the arid yellow of the landscape. The main entrance way standing on the Hill of São Bento is of fabulous Manueline style, opening into a game reserve with an eighteen kilometre perimeter, playground of a luxury-loving dynasty.

Construction of the Paço Ducal was begun in 1501 by Duque Dom Jaime its design reflecting the aesthetic taste of the day. Despite the fact that work was not completed until much later the overall harmony of the building was in no way impaired. The façade, however, is outstanding in the coherence of its twenty three meticulously aligned windows. The entire exterior façade was lined with the famous local Montes Claros marble.

And this is not the full extent of the Vila Viçosa's cultural heritage. But it is up to the visitor to draw up an itinerary which must at all costs, however, include the XIII century castle, the museum and library of the Paço Ducal (XVI and XVIII centuries) the church and cloister of the **Convento das Chagas,** the **Igreja dos Agostinhos** (Augustinian order) and the **Igreja da Esperança** with its XVI century frescos. And then, of course, the discovery of hidden details apparent only to the most attentive eye above and beyond such a wealth of artistic treasures.

ARRAIOLOS

Rising unexpectedly out of the plain, Arraiolos is composed of a series of white rows of houses characterized by their austere façades and broad chimneys, low rooms entered by way of a small flight of steps. The town spreads over a flat area and then extends up the side of a hill on the crown of which a castle was built in 1306. The walled area contains what remains of the original town of Arraiolos, the **Igreja do Salvador,** later superceded in im-

The interior of the Palace of the Dukes of Bragança.

Arraiolos, well-known for its hand-embroidered carpets.

portance by the new **Igreja Matriz**, raised outside the walls when the town spread beyond the limits of the medieval fortifications.

Nowadays, the life of the town goes on outside the walled area, contrary to life in the Middle Ages. The **Igreja da Misericórdia** and the **Espírito Santo Hospital** are sited here, also the **Casa dos Arcos** and the **Casa do Capitão-Mor**, the former situated in the street of the same name and one-time residence of the Counts of Arraiolos, the latter of XVIII century construction. Scattered among the streets are scenes from the Stations of the Cross and the Passion of Christ which are almost overwhelmed by the baroque style of the churches. Everywhere are to be seen small shops displaying the famous Arraiolos carpets, hand embroidered in the most varied of hues. This art was originally introduced by the Moors during the time of their occupation of the Iberian Peninsula. The motifs range from flowers, palms, clouds and animals without number, branches of luxuriant foliage. All scenes embroidered patiently by the women who may be seen by the visitor in the late afternoon working patiently in their doorways.

BEJA

The town occupies the highest hill of the region, offering a fine, sweeping view from its crown which, some would have it extends to the Palmela hills near the sea. The entire area is taken up with whitewashed houses, interspersed with gardens lending breathing space to the earth which has long been tortured by the unremitting sun.

Beja enjoys an enviable collection of monuments, in particular **the castle** and its keep, the **Igreja de Santo Amaro**, the **Roman arch of the Avis gates** and the **Mosteiro da Conceição** housing the **Museu da Rainha Dona Leonor**. Barely ten kilometres distant, on the road to Santa Vitória to the west, are the **Pisões ruins**, an ancient Roman town dating from the I century with panels of beautiful mosaics giving pride of place to flora and fauna, in addition to the classical geometric designs. Further south, close to the Spanish border, is **Mértola** — and the neighbouring towns of **Pomarão, Espírito Santo, Alcaria Ruiva** — of unrivalled panoramic interest.

Beja: the tower of the Castle; below: the interior of the Church of the Old Convent of the Conceiçao, which is now Rainha D. Leonor Museum.

Two views of the towers of Beja; the pastures in the country and a view of the church of Mértola, at sunset.

The wild beauty of the coast of Algarve.

ALGARVE

VILA DO BISPO

North of Sagres lies Vila do Bispo with its beaches of alternating rock and sand, including such names as **Ponta Ruiva, Barriga, Castelejo and Cordama**. A little further afield, Aljezur, between green fields and the mysterious lines of its ruined castle, a town of many bridges and unforgettable walks to the coast. Near the sea are natural look out points offering views of deserted beaches, Penedo da Agulha, ponta da Rocha, Penduradoiro, **Ponta da Atalaia** facing towards a tiny island crowned by the silhouette of an ancient fortress.

The sea coast here is very different from that of the Algarve closer to the Spanish border. The endless stretches of sand to the East make it almost impossible to distinguish where one beach ends and the next begins. The coastline to the west however is different again, in that each beach is flanked by cliffs, serving as borderlines between the villages which cling precariously to the rock to save themselves from being swallowed by the sea.

Everything is of fascinating interest. For instance, the various caves of the Monte Francês on the road from Sagres to Vila do Bispo tempt you to minor speleological expeditions and the wall of dunes stretching far north offer unique panoramas, the most impressive perhaps that to be viewed from the **Torre de Aspa**, the highest cliff of the entire Algarve coast. From this 156 metre perch, the ocean never looked so immense and the waves so undaunting since from this height they no longer appear to be rearing swirls of crashing foam but merely white frothy lines dissolving almost soundlessly on contact with the rocks. This permanently agitated part of the ocean contains the various species of seafood constituting the basis of local cuisine: mussels (mexilhão), barnacles (percebes), rock-bass (robalo), sea-bream (pargo) and anchovies (anchovas).

Beyond, are the beaches of Odeceixe, Almograve and Zambujeira, finest sand protected by rock formations and white villages beside the great ocean. Then follows **Vila Nova de Mil Fontes**, with its river and sea beaches. These are places where the natural local beauty remains intact, a rugged land in permanent altercation with the Atlantic, a pitiless and harsh immensity.

The small port of Sagres at dawn.

A typical house of Vila do Bispo.

Lagos seen from the sea, and part of the port.

LAGOS
SAGRES

Sagres is evocative by definition, past events that the cliffs certainly remember, the **School of Henry the Navigator** (Infante Dom Henrique) with the scant shadow cast by the sun almost overhead reflected on the rocky ground, crows hanging in the air, related perhaps to those which guided São Vicente's body through the waters to Lisbon.

The fort impassively listens to the sounds coming from afar, of an Algarve given over to tourism, beaches filled with people throughout the summer months. **Lagos** close by with its plentiful sands and beautiful **Igreja de Santo António** displaying the wealth of its carved and gilded interior, the Praça da República and the arches of the **Mercado dos Escravos** (slave market). Boat expeditions along the coast depart from the harbour to explore the series of caves worn into the cliff face by the tides, tiny coves protected from the wind, tunnels directing the light in unexpected ways. An obligatory and memorable trip indeed.

Praia Dona Ana and the evocative Ponta de Piedade.

Portimão: two views of the port, one of the liveliest ones of Algarve.

PRAIA DA ROCHA
PORTIMÃO

The lay-out of parts of Portimão even today hark back to a history as remote as the days when the Carthaginians sought Atlantic stopping places, beyond the Mediterraean dominions from which they came. During those times, Portimão was named Portus Hannibalis. Contemporary buildings and the overall physiognomy of the place, however, give no hint of that distant past. Nonetheless, the Moorish influence is very marked in the house fronts, in the popular quarters with their tiles and friezes and porcelain balustrades. The trawlers unloading their day's catch lend constant movement to the estuary banks and, in the distance, **Ferragudo** offers a contrasting atmosphere of deliberately assumed silence and tranquility.

One of the best-known beaches of Portugal lies close to the city, bearing the name dictated by nature: Praia da Rocha — Rock Beach — on account of the strangely-shaped rocks abounding in the area and which have been given names such as os Dois Irmãos (Two Brothers), os Trés Ursos (Three Bears), Rochas Furadas (Pierced Rocks). There is a unique series of small coves stretching all the way to **Alvor**, numerous nooks where the age-old pounding of the sea has driven tunnels and caves into the cliff face in which water and light play with the colours borne of the sun's reflections.

137

ALBUFEIRA
VILAMOURA

Here, the Moorish influence is abundantly obvious: the names, structures and colours of the area are all characteristic of the North African cultural tradition. Nowadays, the region is given over to tourism, a dizzying succession of holiday villages, hotels, marinas and other facilities designed exclusively over the decades to render the visitor's stay yet more agreeable. Vilamoura is a case in point. Nonetheless, the past is still apparent in the cultural tradition of ornamental chimney pots, flat roof terraces, small windows to keep the heat at bay. Albufeira is a white town against an invariably blue sky, extending to the very edge of the cliff as though desiring to throw itself into the sea to escape the torturous heat.

A must in Albufeira is to walk the maze of streets and alleys, go to the beach, relax in one of the numerous open-air cafes, explore by boat and hear the sea noises echoing around the caves dug into the cliffs by time, as at **Ponte Grande**, at **Cova do Xorino**, close encounters with an enchanting and ever-dazzling nature.

The main traits of the Church of Albufeira and an unusual view of the beach.

*The small harbour and a
golf-course of Vilamoura.*

139

MONCHIQUE

The traveller heading south is confronted by the Serra de Monchique, of almost 900 metres in height, as by an oasis created by divine hand for the sole purpose of reviving strength and providing respite for the tired eye in the vast green expanse rendering a welcome break from the monotonous and interminable wheatfields of the Alentejo. Monchique is an old town with a history dating back to the conquest of the Iberian Peninsula by the Romans who here discovered, in the Serra de Monchique, the thermal springs which were later to be frequented by King João II of Portugal and the kingdom's aristocracy.

The visitor will certainly find Monchique one of the most pleasant spots in the Algarve: the town is relatively close to the coast while the woodland air contrasts with the heat of the seaside resorts further south. The town has retained its original appearance, its white walls enlivened by bands of bright colour ranging from ochre, blue and red. Streets winding downhill open into simple squares, lanes leading up to views of the horizon, churches and chapels which, though rising above the surrounding buildings on account of their size, are nonetheless of a simplicity which blends with the whole.

The Serra de Monchique and, below, the beach of Praia da Rocha.

FARO

This is the capital of the Algarve, an honour deriving not only from tradition but also from the extent of its economic activities.

There is no shortage of churches: **Igreja do Carmo**, a major baroque church lying on the northern outskirts; the **cathedral** in the Largo da Sé, the original of which was destroyed in the earthquake of 1755 and now incoporates a series of the different styles in vogue during successive renovations. And many more, of restrained architectural and decorative appearance, offering a welcome haven of cool on hot summer days: **the churches of São Pedro, Misericórdia, São Francisco** and others, attesting to the long-standing religious conviction of the local inhabitants.

The city also offers the visitor other points of interest: the **Alameda de São João de Deus**, the arched gateway of the **Arco da Vila** near the yacht harbour, the Praça Alexandre Herculano with its urban palaces, the various pedestrian streets dominated by brisk trade. For the livelihood of this city derives from the people who visit it. Faro in turn offers peaceful spots, wooded avenues, wrought iron windows overlooking the estuary, beaches intersected by narrow canals inhabited by snipe, herons and storks.

The façade and the interior of the Church do Carmo.

TAVIRA

It is a different Algarve which awaits the visitor here. Paths along the banks of the peaceful river, the centre revealing a desire to be cosmopolitan, the band stand beneath the palms of the public gardens, the palaces, the 37 churches presiding over all since the town first came into being. The most beautiful of them is perhaps that of **Santa Maria do Castelo**, built over a former mosque which is still apparent in the layout of this old church, in addition to the beautiful tiles brought to the Peninsula by the Moorish influence. Nothing now remains of the castle but isolated sections of the walls which time is patiently eroding. From afar — a walk through the countryside is definitely worthwhile — Tavira looks even prettier, the town spilling lazily down the hillside, the church cupolas crowning the assembly of white houses, the entire town decked in almond blossom.

VILA REAL DE SANTO ANTONIO

Spain lies just across the river which, since time immemorial, has divided the two countries. And this geographical location influences every aspect of the life of the local people. Business from over the border and the fact of being a point of transit have brought a little added activitiy to a town which was born to be peaceful. Once the town centre and parish church have been examined, the visitor still has another obligatory place of call: the trip to Monte Gordo in one of the surviving local carriages by way of the road cutting through the dense vegetation along the coast. This is effectively one of the extreme ends of the Algarve for, just across the Guadaina, the countryside might look similar, but it is a different country. And Vila Real de Santo António likewise marks the very tip of Portugal for anyone travelling from north to south.

Tavira: a view of the city and the interior of the Church of the Misericórdia.

Vila Real de Santo António: a picture of local handcraft.

A view of the Praça do Marquês de Pombal.

CONTENTS